D1231814

WAITING
TO DERAIL

WAITING TO DERAIL

RYAN ADAMS AND WHISKEYTOWN, ALT-COUNTRY'S BRILLIANT WRECK

THOMAS O'KEEFE WITH JOE OESTREICH

Skyhorse Publishing

Skyhorse Publishing books may be purchased in bulk at special discounts for sales promotion, corporate gifts, fund-raising, or educational purposes. Special editions can also be created to specifications. For details, contact the Special Sales Department, Skyhorse Publishing, 307 West 36th Street, 11th Floor, New York, NY 10018 or info@skyhorsepublishing.com.

Skyhorse® and Skyhorse Publishing® are registered trademarks of Skyhorse Publishing, Inc.®, a Delaware corporation.

Visit our website at www.skyhorsepublishing.com.

10 9 8 7 6 5 4 3 2 1

Library of Congress Cataloging-in-Publication Data is available on file.

Cover design by Rain Saukas
Cover photo credit: Thomas O'Keefe

Print ISBN: 978-1-5107-2493-8
Ebook ISBN: 978-1-5107-2494-5

Printed in the United States of America

For Stephanie and Sophie

Table of Contents

PROLOGUE

SEATTLE, WASHINGTON. FEBRUARY 1998

A gaggle of cops stood on the sidewalk in front of the hotel, blocking the door to the bus. I flashed my laminate, told them I was the tour manager, and climbed aboard. It was 4:00 a.m., and the front lounge was packed: the whole band, a few EMTs, another cop or two. And there was Ryan Adams, passed out on the couch, being attended to by one of the technicians.

The EMT bent over Ryan and slapped a blood pressure cuff on him. This woke him up a bit, and he seemed to almost register what was happening. He opened one eye, glanced at the tech and the pressure cuff, and said, "Get the fuck off of my bus."

"Ryan, don't talk to these guys like that," said Caitlin Cary, the fiddle player. "They're trying to help you."

Ryan's head wobbled like a newborn baby's, as if his neck were barely strong enough to carry the weight of everything rolling around up there. "Get the fuck off of my bus," he spat out a second time.

The technician spent a few minutes checking Ryan's vitals, and Ryan giggled and babbled and insisted that the authorities get the fuck off his bus. Meanwhile, the rest of us told the EMTs what little we knew about the combination of intoxicants Ryan might have taken. Tomorrow we were playing Vancouver, and because we would soon meet the Canadian drug dogs at the border crossing, we had already cleaned the bus of illegal substances. Tonight's show had ended just five hours earlier, but that seemed like a week ago.

As the technician unfastened the pressure cuff, he said to us, "He's coming out of it. The worst is over." Then he turned back to Ryan and said, "Before we go, I gotta ask you a few questions."

"That's cool," Ryan said.

"Ryan, what city are you in right now?"

"Seattle," he said, slurring the *t*'s right out of the word.

"And where are you from?"

"North Carolina."

"Good. Now can you tell me what day of the week it is?"

"Whoa, whoa," I said. "Hold on a minute. That's not fair. None of us can answer that. We're on tour. Every day is Monday, every day is Friday." I looked at the EMT and shook my head. "Next question."

The tech quizzed him a little longer, and although Ryan could barely get the words out, he'd aced the test so far. "Ryan," the tech said, "Who's the president of the United States?" This was the big money question. Final jeopardy.

Ryan elbowed himself higher. "It's Bill Clinton," he said, "and let me tell you something about Bill Clinton." The Monica Lewinsky scandal had broken a few months earlier, and back in those days Ryan's politics leaned toward the right. "He . . . he . . . he should be in *jail*."

The technician started putting his supplies back into his gear box "Well, Ryan," he said, "at least we agree on one thing."

The EMT and I walked off the bus, and we stood down on the blacktop next to the cops, all of us lit up by the police cruisers and the ambulance. I thanked everybody for their help.

"Goddamn, son," one of cops said. He was an older guy who'd clearly seen his share of criminal mischief in his years on the force. He looked at me and then he turned back toward the bus. "I wouldn't trade jobs with you for anything."

PART

1

THE SHERIFF OF WHISKEYTOWN
(SPRING 1997–FALL 1997)

CHAPTER

1

Nine months earlier, in May of 1997, I got the call that would change my life. It was from a guy who introduced himself as Chris Roldan. Along with his partner, Jenni Sperandeo, he ran Jacknife, an indie promotion company based in Austin. Jacknife's core business, Roldan told me, was radio promotion: helping record labels get their bands played on the airwaves. But recently he and Sperandeo had made the move into artist management. Jacknife's first signing was an act from Raleigh, North Carolina, a band called Whiskeytown, fronted by twenty-two-year-old wunderkind Ryan Adams.

Talking to Roldan that day, I was standing in my kitchen, which was also in Raleigh. A year earlier I had moved to North Carolina's capital city from Charlotte, where I'd spent a decade in a punk rock band called ANTiSEEN. We'd toured extensively through the United States and Europe, and we'd released a bunch of albums, EPs, and singles. I was the bass player, but I also booked the hotel rooms, settled up with the promoters, and made sure everybody showed up on time for sound check. I eventually learned that in the music business, this kind of cat wrangling came with a job title: Tour Manager. After quitting ANTiSEEN and moving to Raleigh, I began to parlay my road experience into a burgeoning career tour-managing other acts. And that—my tour-managing résumé—is what Roldan was calling to talk about. He and Sperandeo were looking for somebody in Raleigh, somebody on the ground, to shepherd Ryan and the band through their next touring cycle.

Whiskeytown had recently signed with Outpost, an imprint of Geffen Records. And they'd just finished recording their major-label debut in Nashville and Los Angeles with producer Jim Scott, known for his work with Tom Petty, Sting, Johnny Cash, and alt-country darlings Wilco. The Whiskeytown record, *Strangers Almanac*, would be released in July. Buzz was already building thanks to the band's 1996 indie release *Faithless Street*, prominent showcases at the SXSW and CMJ music festivals, and the ensuing label courtship in which Outpost emerged the lucky suitor. Ryan and Whiskeytown were now on the launchpad. All systems go. All lights green. Roldan was hoping I could tour-manage the blastoff.

I'd heard of Whiskeytown, of course. By 1997 everybody even remotely connected to the booming Raleigh-Durham-Chapel Hill music scene had heard of Whiskeytown. And most everybody had a story about a run-in with Ryan Adams. Lots of those stories started with a line like *I swear, that kid whines like an eighth-grade girl* or *Bastard owes me twenty bucks*. But nearly every story—even when coming from the Triangle's most jaded scenesters— ended with something to the effect of *You gotta admit, he's pretty goddamn good*.

At that point I'd never seen Ryan on stage—not with Whiskeytown, who'd been together since late 1994, and not with Patty Duke Syndrome, the band he'd formed back in his hometown of Jacksonville, North Carolina, and then reconstituted after moving west to Raleigh. But I had seen him around town, mostly at 7 Even, a North Carolina State University-area convenience store that was every musician's first choice for beer and cigarettes. Standing in front of the coolers, lit up by the overhead fluorescence, Ryan looked like a South-of-the-Mason-Dixon Paul Westerberg—all mussed-up hair and wrinkled clothes. With his big black glasses, he also looked like Austin Powers, and by then a few local musicians had started knocking on Ryan by referring to him as Mike Myers's character. Like me, they'd see him at 7 Even, doing something as mundane as trying to decide between Budweiser and Heineken. One would elbow the other: *Get a load of fucking Powers over there.*

I figured that most of the negativity toward Ryan was the product of envy. In any music scene, when one band gets signed, fifty get jealous. Whiskeytown had been together for less than three years. Ryan was barely over drinking age. He already had a fat record deal, a big-time producer, and the right indie-cool managers. He'd gone straight from rookie ball to the big leagues. Instant success always gets people talking, and the talk around Raleigh that spring was that Ryan Adams was half genius, half jackass.

Now, on the phone, Chris Roldan was telling me just how volatile Ryan could be. He said that during Whiskeytown's most recent string of shows—on the *No Depression* tour, sharing the stage with the Old 97's, Hazeldine, and the Picketts—Ryan and the band had been woefully inconsistent. They would play a tight set of stellar songs one night and then be drunk and sloppy the next. Apparently before the tour was finished, they pulled a U-turn and retreated home to Raleigh, canceling the last few dates without first bothering to call Jacknife or the booking agent to let them know. To hell with the rest of the gigs. Whiskeytown was fed up and worn out, after a mere ten shows or so.

Waiting to Derail

I was a punk rock guy. With ANTiSEEN I'd released records with titles like *Raw Shit* and *Southern Hostility*, so I admired the rebellious spirit of a band saying, "Fuck it." But I knew that the combination of "Fuck" and "It" was the last thing corporate labels wanted to hear from their acts. I also knew that if Ryan was as good as the hype suggested, then his songs deserved better treatment. His fans deserved better. His bandmates deserved better.

The job—if Roldan officially offered it to me and if I took it—would be to make sure that Ryan, for all his self-destructive tendencies, stopped pulling stupid stunts like canceling tours halfway through. The band was young and, as a touring outfit, almost comically green. With a new album in the offing and a bunch of dates on the board, they needed, Roldan said, a big brother. An adult to show them how this whole touring-in-support-of-a-major-label-release thing was supposed to go.

I was pretty sure I could do it. I was thirty-three years old. If not a full-on adult, then certainly adult*ish*. And I had some solid roadwork under my belt. Not only had I played a ton of gigs with ANTiSEEN, I'd also spent most of 1996 tour-managing Lustre, a North Carolina-based alt-rock band that had signed with A&M. I got that gig because their drummer was Greg Clayton, brother of ANTiSEEN frontman Jeff Clayton. After steering Lustre through a long stretch of rock clubs and radio festivals, I spent the fall and winter home in Raleigh, delivering pizzas, trying to track down my next tour-managing gig. I'd come to realize how much I truly enjoyed planning the tour, dealing with the venues, and making sure the shows went well. In the early ANTiSEEN days, back when I was just the bass player, I felt like I was only of use during the one hour I was standing on stage. But as tour manager, I contributed all day long. Now I was anxious to get back on the road. And I was finding out that getting the second job is one of the hardest things to do in the music business—in *any* aspect of show business. Because your first gig, somebody gives you. The second gig, you've got to win on your own.

I made call after call to contact after contact before finally joining up with New York punks D Generation on the last leg of their *No Lunch* tour. I was already a big D Gen fan because they were the perfect fusion of two of my favorite bands, the Ramones and Cheap Trick. Plus they were fun, hilarious guys, so my time with them barely felt like work. But most important, I'd established a track record. When Jacknife started searching for a local tour manager for Whiskeytown, Roldan called Lustre's manager Shawn Rogers, whose office was in Chapel Hill. Rogers recommended me, and now here I was, interviewing for the job, glad that I could answer yes to all Rodan's questions. *Have you ever taken a band through Europe? Ever dealt with Canadian Customs? Ever done an in-studio at a radio station?* Yes, yes, and yes.

After about a half hour, he asked me, "How much does a guy like you charge?"

I had no idea. There's no rulebook for this stuff. No union pay scale. With Lustre I'd gotten like $350 a week. With D Gen, it was maybe a little more. I looked around the house that my longtime girlfriend Stephanie and I were renting. Yep. Adultish. Real furniture, a fireplace, the fridge stocked with food. A television tuned to CNBC. My hair—which used to hang past my shoulders—now cut short. I was damn near domesticated. Crossing my fingers, I said, "Seven hundred?"

"Sounds good," Roldan said without missing a beat.

Fuuuucccck. I should have asked for a thousand. But still, I was fired up. I'd landed my third gig. Three's not a fluke; three's a pattern.

Standing in my kitchen that day, I knew I was lucky that work had found me. All I had to do was pick up the phone. What I didn't know was that Ryan Adams and the band would consume the next three years of my life. Only three people on the planet would witness every single show on the *Strangers Almanac* tour: Ryan Adams, Caitlin Cary (the fiddle player), and me. And of the three of us, I'd be the only one sober enough to remember it all. My experience with Ryan would lead to twenty-plus years tour-managing bands like Train, Third Eye Blind, and Weezer. And Whiskeytown would propel Ryan toward a solo career that would bring multiple Grammy nominations and position him as the heir apparent to Bob Dylan. ("The Next Dylan," of course, is a noose that nobody—not Springsteen, not Adams—enjoys being hung with.)

As I said good-bye to Roldan, I didn't see any of that coming. I just knew I'd lined up a job. And that job consisted of one core mission: get Ryan and the band to the shows and through the shows, all in the name of helping him live up to his talent and to the major-label break he'd been given. I was now the conductor, charged with keeping Whiskeytown on the tracks.

This was a mission I'd prove mostly successful at. Mostly. Not totally. As I would soon learn, 90 percent of the time I could talk Ryan into doing the right thing. Five percent of the time, I could cover up whatever idiotic thing he'd done. But that final 5 percent?

We were fucked.

A week after accepting the job, I saw firsthand why Jacknife needed a local tour manager to handle Whiskeytown. Ryan had overslept, snoozing through some obligation or another. I don't remember the specific responsibility he'd blown off, but it was probably a phone interview with a magazine or newspaper, advance promotion for a minirun of dates that would start in early June. So once again, I got a call from Jacknife in Austin: *We can't get Ryan to answer his phone. Can you head over to his place?*

Like most major colleges, the NC State campus is bordered by a main drag of businesses catering to students. Dive bars with pitcher specials. Pizza. Gyros. Takeout Chinese. Patchouli-smelling headshops and pre-Starbucks coffee shops. Used bookstores and record stores. In Columbus, the main drag is High Street. In Madison, it's State Street. In Boulder, Pearl Street. As I drove from my house to Ryan's apartment that day, I turned onto Raleigh's college strip, Hillsborough Street.

My place was near the eastern end of Hillsborough, between campus and the capitol building. Ryan was living just off the far west end, out by Meredith College in a neighborhood called University Park. Rolling down Hillsborough, I passed Sadlack's Heroes, the sandwich shop/music venue/old-man bar where Ryan drank (often) and worked (sometimes); Schoolkids Records, the archetypal college record store and unofficial hub of the scene; and the Brewery, the rock club that would host Whiskeytown's *Strangers Almanac* album release show at the end of July.

I pulled up to the address Jacknife had given me: 70 Montgomery Street, a one-story brick building that contained five or so apartment units. From the outside, the place was pleasant: corner lot, tree-lined street, just a block off Hillsborough. But pleasant or not, this scene wasn't most people's idea of what just-signed-a-major-label-deal looked like. There was no Mercedes SL-500 parked out front. Nothing you'd call glamorous or even slacker-cool. Still, I'd been around enough newly signed bands to know that more often than not, college-ghetto-grade housing *is* what the major-label dream looked like—until that elusive first hit song.

I walked up the steps and banged on the door. Eventually Ryan answered, looking like I'd just woken him. Because I had. "Hey, man," he said, squinting his eyes to the daylight. And then he let me in.

In the week since Rodan hired me, the only significant time I'd spent with Ryan and the band was a couple days earlier at one of their practices. They rehearsed downtown, near the bus station in an old warehouse that the owner—Van Alston, who also ran one of Ryan's favorite drinking spots, the Comet Lounge—had segmented into several individual practice spaces. It was there that I finally met Ryan and the other band members, most significantly Caitlin Cary and Phil Wandscher. I could immediately tell that Caitlin's fiddle playing and harmony vocals were defining elements of Whiskeytown's sound. And in addition to her vital musical role, she played the part of big sister to Ryan, quick to roll her eyes and huff with frustration when the kid wouldn't quit dicking around. Phil, I soon learned, was like Ryan's fist-fighting, guitar-slinging brother. A talented songwriter, his guitar playing neatly complemented Ryan's—like Ronnie Wood to Ryan's Keith Richards. But it was also clear that Phil was a key contributor to all the aforementioned dicking around. To cop a phrase that Pete Townshend once used to describe Keith Moon, Phil was "a great joiner-inner."

That day at rehearsal, the band did a lot of drinking and smoking but not much actual playing. The ever-professional Caitlin wanted to practice, of course. So did Chris Laney, the new bass player who was still trying to get up to speed on the songs. Drummer Steven Terry, a good-natured, testosterone-driven West Virginian, also wanted to pick up the sticks and get to rocking. He was pretty much always game.

So three-fifths of Whiskeytown were ready to go, but Ryan and Phil looked bored, like they had better things to do. They didn't act like they were just a few weeks from hitting the road in support of a big-time record, and they didn't act as if they were trying to impress the new tour manager. They were half-assing practice like they were already as huge as the Rolling Stones.

In between songs, during the extended drinking and smoking intermissions, Ryan asked me questions—but it wasn't a job-interview kind of back-and-forth like I'd had a few days earlier with Roldan. Ryan's questions were more like, "What's your favorite color?" Real off-the-wall stuff.

Still, over the next hour, Ryan put it together that I'd been in ANTiSEEN. As a teenager he'd listened to our records. He may have even seen us live. And now, learning that I had played in a band he dug, he became more focused than I'd seen him all night. The dicking around stopped. No more oddball questions. Suddenly he was as earnest and curious as an AP History student, asking about the bands we had toured with, about the shows I'd seen. In between drags on his cigarette, he would nod and say, "Wow, man. Cool."

Ryan was raised in eastern North Carolina, in Jacksonville, home of Marine Corps Base Camp Lejeune. The Onslow County air was scented with magnolia blossoms and whole hog BBQ. Fertile ground for country music. But he'd grown up riding skateboards and buying Black Flag records. Ryan Adams, the up-and-coming alt-country poster boy, was at heart a punk rock kid like me.

From the late-seventies onward, lots of bands—both in the South and nationally—had played some strain of twangy punk or punky twang. Just for starters, think: the Blasters, X, the Georgia Satellites, Dash Rip Rock, the Supersuckers, and my personal favorites, Jason & the Scorchers. But by the midnineties, the merging of country and punk had started to swell into a movement. It was going by many different names (alternative country, insurgent country, Americana, cowpunk, roots rock, twangcore, y'alternative), but it had one bible: *No Depression* magazine, named for the first album by the quintessential alt-country band Uncle Tupelo. Applying a label to an artistic movement can be tricky; art is slippery and not easily categorized. Maybe "cowpunk" best describes a country-influenced punk band, while "alt-country" is the term for a punk-influenced country band. But whatever order you put the two components in, for an increasing number of acts, combining country and punk made sense because it mirrored the diversity of their record collections. They dug George Jones *and* the Ramones. The Carter Family *and* the Clash. Alt-country was built on the same logic as the Reese's Peanut Butter Cup: *I like both things separately. They're probably even better if I put 'em together.*

By the time I started with Whiskeytown, alt-country acts were not only filling college bars and punk clubs; they were catching the ear of the music industry. Uncle Tupelo had already split into Wilco and Son Volt, and both offshoots had signed with major labels. The Jayhawks and the Bottle Rockets had already released multiple big-label albums. Veteran songwriters like Steve Earle and Lucinda Williams were getting press, not in country publications but in slick rock magazines like *Rolling Stone* and *Spin*. Even here locally, in the Triangle, bands like the Backsliders and 6 String Drag were building nice followings—and collecting the business cards of A&R reps.

Despite the growing industry attention, alternative country hadn't yet crossed into the mainstream the way that, ten years earlier, alternative rock had. By the midnineties, the biggest alt-rock acts (Smashing Pumpkins, Rage Against the Machine, etc.) had become rock's biggest acts, period. But alt-country was still simmering underground, being played in places like the 40 Watt in Athens and the 7th Street Entry in Minneapolis—the same venues that had given rise to R.E.M., the Replacements, and the first wave of alt-rock. But if the major labels had a say in it, alt-country was ready to move from fringe to front-and-center.

During the 1996 SXSW music festival, at a panel called "Americana," industry insiders spoke at length, according to the *Austin Chronicle*, about how "insurgent country [would] be the genre with a bullet in 1996." One of the panelists was Jenni Sperandeo from Jacknife, and she said there was "a list of bands as long as [her] arms" that were merging country and punk. The larger question for the panel—and the music business as a whole—was how to get this newly hot genre into the hands of record buyers. Alt-country may have had its practitioners, its bible, and its core audience of true believers, but in order for the movement to become as mainstream as alt-rock, it needed the right vehicle—its own Michael Stipe and R.E.M., its own Kurt Cobain and Nirvana—to carry the message out of the underground clubs and up to the masses. Reprise Records was betting on Jeff Tweedy and Wilco. Elektra Records was betting on Rhett Miller and the Old 97's. And Outpost Records was betting on Ryan Adams and Whiskeytown.

So now, a few days after that half-assed practice, I was walking into Ryan's apartment, on my assignment to get him up and running for the phoner. His place was tiny. Dripping with dirty clothes. There must have been a bed, but I don't think there was a TV. Instead, I saw a big ashtray filled with cigarette butts. A bunch of empty beer cans. It smelled like a bar at last call. On the coffee table were compact discs and dog-eared books. Lying on the couch, a couple guitars.

And paper. Everywhere, paper. Bar napkins, notepads, pages torn from journals and composition binders. All with lyrics and drawings scribbled on them.

If you were to peek through the window at the debris, you might assume a hobo was squatting at 70 Montgomery. But starting that day, and over the course of the next few weeks as I got to know Ryan better, it became obvious that the kid was a true artist. A single-minded student of rock-and-roll music. He seemed to have no concern for anything except songs, bands, and rock stories. He didn't have hobbies. He didn't follow sports. He didn't care about money. He didn't talk all that much about girls—except for an occasional mention of an ex-girlfriend named Melanie. Music was all he gave a shit about, all he did. There was also the drinking and smoking, of course, but Ryan really only cared about those vices in the context of their place in the rock-and-roll aesthetic. If Keith Richards drinks and smokes and takes drugs—well then, that's what you do. Ryan, I now understood, wasn't influenced by the sound of punk so much as the defiant attitude. Band practice? Phone interviews with newspapers? Fuck 'em.

I eventually got him on the phone for the interview, but first we spent an hour continuing the conversation we'd started a few days earlier at rehearsal. Bands we both loved. Mutual friends we had. He was a D Generation fan, and he'd recently been introduced to their singer Jesse Malin and guitarist Danny Sage by the A&M Records rep Debbie Southwood-Smith. Because I'd just come off the road with D Gen, I had a hundred great stories, and it seemed like Ryan wasn't going to get on the phone until I told him all of them. Then we talked Ramones and Black Sabbath. And why Black Flag's *Slip It In* totally rules. Ryan never mentioned the term alt-country once, which was fine by me. At that time, my knowledge of the genre was limited. I had heard of Wilco, the Bottle Rockets, and some of the better-known Americana bands, but I wasn't a superfan. I didn't read *No Depression*. Having spent the previous year doing radio station festivals with Lustre, I was much more familiar with the new crop of alt-rock bands, acts like Seven Mary Three, Everclear, and the Nixons. And in my CD player you'd be more likely to find Cheap Trick's *Dream Police* or KISS's first album than anything by the Blood Oranges or Blue Mountain.

Like me, Ryan had only minimal interest in alt-country as a genre. He wanted to talk about bands and songs, not about categories and distinctions. Also like me, Ryan was a high school dropout who'd eventually earned his GED. He may not have brought home a diploma from Jacksonville High, but he'd had a thorough musical education, one that didn't come from textbooks, but from record albums. He'd been schooled at the tip of the phonograph needle.

Reclining James Dean-style on his tattered couch, Ryan was just twenty-two years old, already an expert on the subject of rock and roll. But he and Whiskeytown didn't know spit about being in a touring band. In June, with the release of *Strangers Almanac* just six weeks away, we were going to pack up a van and take the show on the road.

I'd soon find out that the show was a circus.

CHAPTER

Strangers Almanac would be released at the end of July, followed by an all-out, coast-to-coast tour in support of the record. But that was still more than a month away. First we were scheduled to play a handful of warm-up dates, two miniruns spread over a couple of long weekends. Some of the gigs would be high profile, like the slot the band's booking agent, Scott Clayton, had scored at Summerfest in Milwaukee. Others would be in tiny bars, like the date at the end of June in East Lansing, Michigan. Gig number one was a show at Southern Illinois University.

I put together the classic touring band set-up: twelve-passenger rental van, U-Haul trailer swinging off the back. Then we rolled west onto I-40, aiming for Carbondale. Ryan rode shotgun; I was behind the wheel. Everybody else—Caitlin, Phil, Steven, and Chris—tried to get comfortable on the back benches. The only other crew member with us was the soundman, Bruce Neese. With his goth-black clothes and long, dark hair, he looked the opposite of alt-country, like he'd gone AWOL from a Swedish death-metal band. But Bruce hadn't grown up in Örnsköldsvik; he was from Athens, Georgia, and he spoke with an Andy Griffith-sounding accent, patient and even-tempered, which is the exact disposition you need if you hope to survive being sardined in a van with a bunch of stinking, smoking musicians.

Because Ryan and I sat up front, we controlled the stereo, and we immediately tried to educate the backbenchers on the brilliance that is D Generation's *No Lunch* album. But Caitlin, Phil, and the others favored the twang half of the twang-punk merging, and they were not digging the NYC glam rock. Not at all. "Oh, man," I heard somebody say from the back. "What *is* this shit?" I think some of them put on headphones. Or earplugs. Or tried to deep-breathe themselves into a meditative trance. Over on the passenger side, Ryan was banging out air drums.

At this point in his early career, Ryan was in a bind. On the one hand, he was alt-country's savior-of-the-moment, the person best positioned to spread the y'alternative gospel. Trouble was, he didn't want to shoulder the weight of a movement, didn't want to be pigeonholed into a single genre. That very June he told the Cleveland *Plain Dealer* that he hated the alt-country label. "I think it sucks," he said. "We're an American rock n' roll band." He said essentially the same thing to David Menconi, who wrote for the Raleigh *News & Observer* and was an early Ryan Adams champion. "I could give a fuck about being a country band," Ryan told him. "I just want to be a *good* band."

Ryan could bad-mouth the genre all day long, but Whiskeytown was undoubtedly benefiting from the buzz that alt-country had generated among record companies, radio programmers, and music fans. The band got much more ink and attention than they would have if they hadn't been stamped with the label. As the saying goes: a rising tide lifts all boats. And in 1997, the alt-country tide was absolutely on the rise—whether Ryan embraced the term or not.

So even as Ryan was disowning alt-country, he was capitalizing on it. The dude was shrewd enough to work both angles simultaneously.

It had rained earlier in the day, so before we could sound check at Southern Illinois University, we had to ask the landscaping crew if they would jet the water off the stage using their leaf blowers. The stage wasn't a stage-proper; it was the landing at the top of the stairs that led to Shyrock Auditorium. The band would play with their backs to the building, facing out toward a campus-quad greenspace.

After sound check, I tried gathering everybody together so I could pass out the per diems, the forty or so dollars a day allotted for meals and expenses. At per diem time, musicians usually come running like kindergartners to the ice cream man, but Whiskeytown didn't appreciate the enormity of what was happening. I essentially had to talk them into taking the money.

"What's this?" Steven Terry asked me.

I handed him his cash. "Per diem."

He squinted at me like I was speaking Latin. I *was* speaking Latin, but still. These guys had so little road experience; they didn't understand why I was standing there on the campus lawn, passing out free money. It wasn't free, of course. The per diems came out of the tour budget, which was bolstered by the tour support allotment that had been negotiated in the band's contract with Outpost Records . . . but maybe that was more information than the drummer could handle right that minute.

"It's like your lunch money," I said.

Steven looked suspicious, as if the whole per diem deal was too good to be true.

"See that over there?" I pointed toward a steam cart, where a vendor was serving up hotdogs to a line of college kids. "You can take this money and go buy yourself a dog."

It clicked. "Oh. Okay." He lumbered off in that direction.

Eventually they'd all become highly skilled at spending their lunch money, so much so that I'd learn the hard way not to give them a whole week's worth of cash all at once. They'd be broke by Tuesday. Instead, I doled out Friday's per diem on Friday, Saturday's per diem on Saturday, et cetera. I built fiscal restraint right into the system. At that point, Whiskeytown knew almost nothing about touring at the big-league level—which wasn't their fault. They hadn't yet had the opportunity to learn. Unlike most major-label acts that tour their way through the minors before getting signed, these guys had gone straight from the edge of their beds to the bigs without first doing the roadwork. I was going to have to teach them the basics: Don't accept drinks from strangers; try not to drink tap water in city after city; don't tell anybody the name of the hotel you're staying in, and so many other rules of the road. Tour-managing Whiskeytown was going to be like chaperoning eighth graders on a class trip to DC. Eighth graders who drank and smoked pot.

That night in Carbondale, I saw Whiskeytown in front of a legit crowd for the first time. I'd been to their half-assed practices, but this was my first full-tilt show. The first thing I learned is that Ryan might have been the heart of Whiskeytown, but Caitlin Cary was the soul: the melancholy sound of her fiddle, the way her vocal harmonies floated above Ryan's, adding a teaspoon of sugar to the salt-and-snot of Ryan's voice. Ryan had already replaced original drummer Skillet

Gilmore (Caitlin's boyfriend, who, after quitting, had tour-managed Whiskeytown on the *No Depression* tour, the run of shows they gave up on halfway through) and two bass players, Steve Grothmann and Jeff Rice. But there was no replacing Caitlin.

Caitlin had grown up in Seville, Ohio, just outside Akron. After graduating from the College of Wooster and then living for a while in Houston and Richmond, she moved to Raleigh to get her master's in creative writing at NC State. She and Ryan met through Skillet, who was the center of a circle of musicians who all drank and/ or worked at Sadlack's Heroes, the bar on Hillsborough Street. The fiddle player and the young songwriter were a perfect pairing because they weren't an exact match. They were complementary pieces. Caitlin was studying toward a grad degree; Ryan was armed with a GED. She wore short hair and glasses; he wore shaggy sideburns and an old t-shirt. If you walked out of an SIU night class and didn't know better, you might see them standing next to each other on stage—Ryan in the center and Caitlin at stage right—and think a graduate teaching assistant and one of her freshman comp students had formed a band. After that afternoon's confusion with the per diems, I knew that I was going to need Caitlin to help me tutor the rest of the guys in the rock-and-roll seminar that commenced that night in Carbondale: Touring Band 101.

The second thing I learned was that Whiskeytown in a live setting could legitimately rock. On songs from *Strangers Almanac* like "Waiting to Derail" and "Yesterday's News," they *crushed*. I may have been a grizzled punk veteran, but there were times when I got goose bumps—and not from the cool of Carbondale June. The trouble was, as soon as the band built up a head of steam, the energy would always dissipate in the drawn-out breaks they took between songs. They would play a tune. The crowd would clap. The clapping would end. And then Ryan would stand there in the silence. Maybe he'd light up a cigarette. Maybe he'd tune his Telecaster. Then they'd spend an awkward minute mumbling back and forth trying to figure out what the next song was going to be. From my spot off the side of the stage, I'd look at my watch, measuring the long minutes. Lots of bands get by just fine without writing up a set list. Whiskeytown wasn't one of them.

At some point in the show, they covered Neil Young's "Helpless," but Ryan made up new words, changing the chorus to *laundry, laundry, laundry, laundry*. The updated verses were an ode to Ryan's dirty clothes, which, as I knew from seeing the inside of his apartment, were majestic in their abundance. *Laundry (x4)*. I chuckled and shook my head. You could take Whiskeytown out of the dick-around practice room, but you couldn't take the dicking around out of Whiskeytown.

From Carbondale we headed to St. Louis—Uncle Tupelo and Bottle Rockets territory—for a show at the High Pointe. Then we steered down to Birmingham and back to Raleigh, where we regrouped for the next minitour, which took us to up to the Great Lakes for gigs in Cleveland, Milwaukee, and East Lansing.

We arrived in Milwaukee the day before our gig at Summerfest, driving in from Cleveland, where the previous night the band had played for a crowd that largely consisted of Caitlin's Ohio family. The *Plain Dealer*'s review of the show said, "Much of it was highly energized and entertaining, but Whiskeytown showed an annoying tendency to get sloppy in places." From the side of the stage, I decided that I'd soon have to give the band some tough love about the need for a set list.

Because we had the night off before the next day's Summerfest gig, we agreed to head over to the festival to soak in the scene. Feel the Lake Michigan breeze, drink a few beers, bang down some fried cheese curds. The problem was we didn't have tickets. If we'd been a more established act, like the Dave Matthews Band or Bush—both of whom were playing the festival that year—we could get passes comped, no problem. But because Whiskeytown was a new band, I needed to go to the office and beg.

We walked about a mile from our downtown hotel to the festival grounds. I found the office, and we all gathered inside the lounge area, which was outfitted with a couch and a few chairs.

"Hi, how you doing?" I said to the woman who was in charge. "We're a band that's playing here tomorrow. The thing is, we got into town early. Any chance we could get passes for tonight?"

I knew it was a tough ask. Summerfest is one of the largest and most prominent music festivals in the world—because of the big name acts it attracts, its long history, and because each year's edition lasts for nearly two weeks. Summerfest started in 1968, and in the years since, it has become a mandatory tour stop for every band notable enough to make the lineup. Stretching from June 26 to July 6, the 1997 event marked the festival's 30th anniversary. It would draw upwards of 750,000 fans and feature hundreds of bands, including the Foo Fighters, No Doubt, Counting Crows, John Mellencamp, and—hot damn—Whiskeytown. Time to see if that carried any weight.

The woman looked over my shoulder and scowled, which confused me. I thought I'd been polite. "Take your feet off there," she said.

I turned around and saw Phil Wandscher, tall and blond, stretched back on the couch, long legs extended, boots on the coffee table.

"You come here asking for tickets and you act like that?" She looked at me and then back to Phil. "This isn't your living room."

Sometimes I think that one of the qualifications for being a guitar player in a rock band *is* seeing the world like it's all your living room. That's how Phil saw it, anyway. The first time I'd met him was earlier that year at a party Greg Clayton was hosting. Greg was Lustre's drummer, and he'd just come off a year on the road. But that night Phil was the one doing the talking. A cocky left-hander, he spent most of the night bragging about the deal Whiskeytown had signed with Outpost, about the new pickup truck he'd just bought, about recording with producer Jim Scott in Nashville and how *Strangers Almanac* was going to be huge.

At some point, the conversation swung to the topic of musicians and tax law. "I don't even save my receipts," Phil said, meaning that he was such a rock star he didn't bother with stuff so pedestrian as itemized deductions.

But for all his talk, he wasn't being especially arrogant. Everything he said was true. He *had* just signed a fat record contract. In fact, Ryan and Phil were the only two band members who had signed it. A year before the Milwaukee show, in the summer of 1996, record companies were in hot and heavy pursuit of Whiskeytown. The labels were still flush with cash in those postgrunge years, partly because consumers had spent the previous decade rebuying on CD the albums they'd originally owned on vinyl. *Digital! It sounds better! It lasts longer! Upgrade your whole collection! . . . Again!* Back then, changes in media format, like from vinyl to cassette to CD, meant more product for fans to buy, which meant more profit for the record companies. The introduction of the CD created an opportunity: labels could sell a million new compact discs of an old album, Van Halen's *Fair Warning*, say, without the expense of signing and developing Van Halen a second time or paying to have those songs rerecorded. All the income, none of the start-up costs. The digital revolution—in the beginning, when it was limited to quaint little compact discs—looked like a goose dropping golden eggs. Now, of course, we know that the digitization of music would lead to file sharing and streaming, to songs and albums (almost) ceasing to exist as physical objects, and to a whole generation that sees music as free rather than for sale. That digital goose would swallow the music industry whole.

But in 1996, the labels still had wallets fat enough to gin up a good, old-fashioned bidding war, and Whiskeytown was one of the bands being fought over. A&R reps would fly to Raleigh for shows, and they'd invite everybody up to New York for meetings and dinners. But then in the restaurant, Ryan would behave like a brat and abruptly scoot his chair back and walk out, which would embarrass Caitlin and frustrate the label rep who had thrown down the AmEx gold card to pay for the meal.

A&M's Debbie Southwood-Smith—who had inked deals with Uncle Tupelo and D Generation—fell for Ryan earliest and hardest. She worked her ass off trying to get him to sign—as a solo act, if that's what it took. Ryan has always said that from the band's inception, he meant for it to be a collection of equals rather than a star frontman with anonymous backing musicians. But given Ryan's personality—not to mention the fact that he wrote and sang nearly all the songs—Whiskeytown was never going to be egalitarian in the way of, say, Fleetwood Mac. No band with Ryan Adams in it could ever be a democracy. Instead, the Whiskeytown dynamic in those early years functioned something like the Replacements: a singing-songwriting prodigy (with Ryan playing the part of Paul Westerberg) standing alongside two primary foils (with Caitlin and Phil being coconspirators in the vein of Bob and Tommy Stinson). Southwood-Smith showed Ryan around New York, letting him crash at her apartment, introducing him to musicians and industry people, including her assistant, Amy, who he quickly developed a crush on. The fact that Southwood-Smith had signed D Gen to their first deal carried a lot of weight with Ryan, and early on, A&M was the clear frontrunner.

But by September, they were competing with Outpost Records, a new label cofounded by A&R executive Mark Williams (who'd played a big part in signing R.E.M. to I.R.S. Records and Smashing Pumpkins to Virgin Records), artist manager Andy Gershon (who'd handled Smashing Pumpkins, Love and Rockets, and the Sundays, among others), and producer Scott Litt (who'd worked with R.E.M. and Nirvana). Backed by Geffen Records, Outpost combined the cool factor of an indie with the resources of a major.

At that time, Skillet was still playing drums and Steve Grothmann was on bass, and all the label attention was starting to cause a strain on a group of personalities that was pretty turbulent to begin with. Skillet was trying to talk Ryan out of even signing with a major label, whispering in his ear that Whiskeytown was a punk band, not a corporate rock band. Just as Skillet was like a minidevil on Ryan's shoulder, pressing him not to sign a corporate deal, Phil was a minidevil sitting on Ryan's other shoulder, urging him *to* scrawl his name on the line. And Phil was adamant that Whiskeytown sign as a *band*—as Ryan had originally intended it to be—not as a solo project.

The whole process stressed them nearly to the breaking point. Frustrated by the tension that the label courtship had already caused—and by Ryan's sophomoric behavior—Caitlin, Skillet, and Steve Grothmann all quit. This left Ryan and Phil as the last two Whiskeytowners standing. And ultimately they decided to go with Outpost. I don't know for certain why they turned away from A&M at the end. It could be that the collective résumé of Williams/Gershon/Litt was so impressive, it outshone even Southwood-Smith's experience with Uncle Tupelo and D Gen. I've also heard about a dinner with A&M that turned sour because the label picked a restaurant that was too yuppie-snooty for Ryan's taste. He walked out before dessert. Whatever the case, Whiskeytown signed with Outpost. Because Phil was the only other band member left, he put his name right under Ryan's. Outpost gave Whiskeytown a record deal. For all Debbie Southwood-Smith's work, all A&M ended up giving Ryan was an introduction to Amy, who would soon become his girlfriend.

Caitlin soon decided that she wanted to come back; she'd worked hard to get to the point where she had a musical stake in Whiskeytown. Ryan and Phil welcomed her, and though she rejoined the band on stage, she was no longer a full member in the legal, contractual sense. She remained, however, a necessary component in the *artistic* sense. Skillet and Steve Grothmann were not as musically necessary. Skillet came back to tour-manage the *No Depression* tour, but he was out as the drummer. Steven Terry took his place behind the kit. Grothmann was replaced on bass by Jeff Rice, who would in turn be replaced by Chris Laney.

By the time we hit Milwaukee, I'd only seen the band play live a handful of times, but I felt like I understood the elemental equations.

Ryan + Caitlin = The Musical Beauty of Whiskeytown.

Ryan + Phil = The Punk Rock Spirit of Whiskeytown.

Waiting to Derail

Here's something else I knew: the band was a three-headed monster, but not all heads were of equal size and importance. Lots of people could make a guitar sound like Phil, but nobody else sounded quite like Caitlin.

At Summerfest, the woman eventually agreed to comp us the passes. I think she took pity on me, recognizing that I was essentially babysitting bad-mannered musicians. Once inside the gates, we walked down the deep-fried midway, and then Ryan and I decided to go check out Seven Mary Three, the band that'd had a huge hit with "Cumbersome." Lustre had opened for them the previous summer, so I was friends with the 7M3 guys, and Ryan and I got to watch the show from the side of the stage. Afterwards, as we headed back to their dressing room, Ryan said, "Yeah, man. Let's go meet Seven Mary *E*." He'd already figured out the grunge-ready key most of their songs were set in.

They must have been playing the Miller-sponsored stage, because in the dressing room there were about a million Genuine Drafts on ice. Ryan and I got busy drinking as many of them as we could. It turned out that Jason Ross, Seven Mary Three's singer, was already a Whiskeytown superfan, and he was excited to meet Ryan. The fact that a platinum-selling musician from beyond the *No Depression*/alt-country world had not only heard of but *loved* Whiskeytown confirmed for me that *Strangers Almanac* could be huge. Jason asked him serious questions about songwriting and about recording with Jim Scott. But Ryan answered by telling Jason how he was going to rip off his own head and kick it around like a soccer ball, how he was going to rip off his own arm and pat himself on the back with it. He was being the same kind of jackass he'd been at band practice, asking me my favorite color. Maybe this was the mode the kid went into when he was nervous.

The whole time he was talking about ripping off his appendages, Ryan had a glob of milkshake stuck in his hair. How he'd achieved this milkshake mousse, I had no idea, but the dude looked like the very hobo you might think was squatting is his apartment back in Raleigh. The Seven Mary Three guys looked at me like, *Who's this lunatic you brought back here?* Still, they laughed it off, and two years later, when 7M3 was playing an alt-rock radio festival in Raleigh, Ryan joined them up on stage to play a few songs.

After Summerfest closed for the night, Ryan and I walked back downtown. A few blocks from our hotel, we came upon the Hilton, where parked out front was a massive, gleaming tour bus. We both— separately, instinctively— stopped on the sidewalk to check it out.

"Man, look at this," I said. "We're gonna rent one of these someday." I explained the little bit I knew about how bus touring works: after the gig, you ride all night. When you wake up, you're in the next town.

Ryan looked at me in disbelief, as if I'd just told him tomorrow's show was on Venus. It didn't seem possible to him that Whiskeytown could ever get tour-bus-big. It was odd: despite how thoroughly he'd considered the creative arc of his career, he hadn't given much thought to the logistics.

Then Kevin Cronin from REO Speedwagon stepped off the bus. Ryan recognized the REO frontman immediately, which speaks to the breadth of his rock-and-roll knowledge. He walked up and introduced himself to Cronin, all traces of the kick-his-own-head-like-a-soccer-ball jackassness gone. Cronin was a supernice guy, good Midwestern stock, and we talked with him for five or ten minutes. After a while, I stood back, kept my mouth shut, and just took in the picture. Cronin was in his midforties, with a dozen or so albums and two number one hits. The veteran. Adams was in his early twenties, a month away from his major-label debut. The rookie.

"I'll tell you what," Cronin said to Ryan. "Why don't you guys stop by our show tomorrow night?"

Ryan smiled and nodded. "That'd be cool."

Cronin then took the lanyard that held his REO *all access* pass, pulled it up over his head, and placed it on Ryan's shoulders.

CHAPTER

3

Whiskeytown's Summerfest gig was in the afternoon on one of the smaller stages in the middle of the grounds—not one of the big anchor stages at the ends of the main artery. Imagine Summerfest as a shopping mall: we weren't playing Macy's; we were playing the Sunglass Hut. Our stage was near the beer trailers and the food stalls, and as we set up the gear, the Lake Michigan breeze carried the smell of sizzling bratwurst and onions. Seagulls looked down from on high.

I could already tell that the crowd would mostly be people walking by on their way to somewhere else. Parents with a cup of beer in one hand, trying to push a stroller with the other. Older folks looking for the country music stage. If Whiskeytown had any chance of holding the audience's attention, they couldn't afford two-minute pauses between songs. They needed a set list. After getting the gear ready, I told them as much.

"But this is how we do it," Ryan said.

I figured they'd fight me. They wanted a sleepy, slacker feel to their shows, nothing overly professional. In alt-country circles, it wasn't cool to look like you'd planned things out in advance. "I'm not asking for much," I said. "Just be in control of your own show instead of 'uh, um, what song are we playing next?'"

Ryan winced. "I don't know, man." You'd think I asked him to change into parachute pants or something.

Chris Laney, the bass player, joined in. "Man," he said to me, "you're trying your turn us into Seven Mary Nixon."

He was combining the band Ryan and I had seen the night before with the Nixons, another act Lustre had played with. It was a funny line. But still, drawing up a set list didn't mean they'd be selling out or sacrificing spontaneity. I just wanted to put an end to the confusion between every song. Those long, silent pauses were boring. I turned toward Ryan and Phil. I think Caitlin had walked away by then. "Let's talk about the Rolling Stones," I said, "your favorite band ever. You think they're too cool to draw up a set list?"

I lost the argument. When the band took the stage, there were maybe thirty people watching. The rest of the audience was walking. Whiskeytown played a couple songs to a smattering of applause that was mostly drowned out by the noise coming from the other stages. Then, during one of the extralong breaks, Phil leaned into his mic and said, "Hey, Milwaukee. What the fuuuuuuuuuucckk is going on?"

I looked down at the second hand on my watch, thinking *Let's see how long 'til I get a tap on the shoulder.*

Sure enough, twenty-five seconds later, the stage manager appeared. "Hey, this is a family event," he said. "Tell that asshole to stop cussing."

I took out a Sharpie and wrote *No Cussing* on a piece of paper, and then I ran up and dropped it at the foot of the stage, right where the set list should have been.

That stretch of dates culminated with—or maybe I should say bottomed out at—a gig in East Lansing, Michigan. Jenni Sperandeo from Jacknife had gone to college at Michigan State, and she, rather than Scott Clayton, the band's booking agent, had lined up this date at her old drinking spot, a joint called Mac's Bar. Jenni was flying up from Austin for the show. She'd planned the perfect homecoming: she and her college friends, hanging out at their favorite bar, watching the kick-ass band she was managing.

These were the days before GPS. You had to plan out your route the old-fashioned way, with a combination of the Rand McNally and chicken-scratched directions. As I steered the van toward the gig, I was assuming that the bar sat near campus, probably smack on MSU's version of Hillsborough St. But my directions led me away from the action, to the west side of I-496. We weren't near the college or the capitol building. We were in the middle of industrial nowhere. Pulling into the lot, I saw that Mac's Bar was tiny, which wasn't necessarily bad, but we'd just finished playing Summerfest, and the contrast between the big-time festival and this small-time tavern was stark. Ryan was irritated before he even got out of the van.

When we stepped inside, everybody's mood darkened. The place had all the trappings of a sports bar, not a rock club. A few townie-looking dudes in ballcaps and jerseys were sucking beers and staring at the Detroit Tigers game that beamed from the TVs behind the bar. The drop ceiling panels were the color of exhaust-grayed hockey ice. The carpet looked like worn AstroTurf.

There was no stage, just a spot in the corner barely large enough for the five band members to stand in. Then our soundman Bruce Neese and I discovered that the PA system couldn't handle a five-piece band. The mixing board had maybe four channels. There were two or three microphones all told. The speakers—smaller than the ones on my home stereo—were propped up on tripod stands. Jenni had booked the gig, but as we loaded in, I knew I was the one who'd fucked up.

At that point, I'd only been tour-managing for a year and a half. Even though I had much more road experience than Whiskeytown, I was still unseasoned. Today, when I advance a show, I spend a few hours on the phone with the promoter, and then I read through pages and pages of sound system amperage, lighting wattage, and other technical data. But in 1997, advancing the show meant calling ahead to get driving directions and set times. Hopefully find out that the band got free beer. That's it. When I advanced the Mac's show, I never thought to ask, "Do you have as many mics as we have mouths?" Lesson learned.

We decided to do the gig half-acoustic, with mics only on the kick drum and vocals, maybe a line for Caitlin's fiddle. Nobody was happy. Whiskeytown was pissed at the club; I was pissed at myself for not sniffing out the inadequacies in advance. Ryan just flat-out didn't want to be there. Sports bars were not his scene.

So he got wasted and belligerent. In addition to Jenni and her friends, the crowd was a mix of alt-country diehards, college kids, and the townie dudes still watching the baseball game. The band played a few songs, and Ryan grew increasingly frustrated with the TV watchers, whose backs were turned to the stage. He tried to get their attention by knocking his guitar out of tune and making an obnoxious Z-minor chord. The dudes at the bar started booing.

Ryan grabbed the mic and said, "Remember that time Earnhardt won the Super Bowl? And he threw that basketball by hitting it with a bat, and it sailed right through the uprights? That was awesome!"

The guys at the bar may have been paying more attention to the game than to the band, but they knew they were being mocked. They unleashed a chorus of fuck-yous. Somebody chucked a handful of ice.

"Fuck this place," Ryan said, taking off his guitar. "You're just the kind of asshole jocks that used to beat up me and my skater friends." He dropped his guitar to the ground with a discordant thud. "I'm fuckin' outta here." He stormed off the stage and headed for the doors.

Now the college kids were booing. Even the alt-country diehards were booing.

The tension followed Ryan outside. It felt like a rumble, like a parking lot brawl straight from *The Outsiders*. Dudes were threatening to kick Ryan's ass. Steven Terry was all bowed up and ready to throw down. Somebody hurled a rock at the van. Somebody else threw a bottle. Ryan, Steven, and Phil fired bottles back.

I had to get the band out of there before one of them got hurt. Bruce Neese and I hustled back inside to grab a load of gear. Luckily, because we'd done the show half-acoustic, there wasn't as much equipment to move out as usual. As I quick-timed from the front door to the "stage," I saw Caitlin sitting at Jenni's table, probably apologizing. When I got back out to the parking lot, Ryan, Steven, and Phil were sitting on top of the van, firing full beer cans at the mob. Phil and Steven were threatening to climb down and kick some ass; dudes standing in the lot were threatening to climb up. *Come on, motherfucker. No, motherfucker. YOU come on.*

With an armful of gear, I tried to play peacemaker—*Hey, now. Break it up*—while simultaneously loading the trailer as fast as I could. Then a car drove by, and somebody tossed tomatoes at us from out the passenger window. How had they managed to get a hold of produce in the middle of a riot? Had they gone grocery shopping?

Finally Norm, the bar manager, came walking out. I was relieved. He'd talk some sense into his people. Meanwhile, the tomato chuckers circled back for another salvo.

"This is bullshit," I said to Norm. "Where's a cop when you need one?"

"Oh, don't worry," he said. "The cops will be here soon. Because I'm about to call them on *you* assholes. For inciting a riot."

In the years since the East Lansing show, I've learned a few things. First I found out that Mac's is technically in Lansing rather than East Lansing, but whatever. More important, I learned that Norm and his business partner, Kenny, were good guys. They booked bands as a labor of love into a place that had been an old-man bar. A bunch of cool Michigan and Midwest bands regularly played Mac's, acts like Bantam Rooster, whom Jack White has cited as an influence. Norm often invited broke touring musicians to crash in his basement, where he would spread out enough couch cushions to accommodate a small platoon. Sleeping on the hard floor of a damp basement sucks, objectively, but that kind of make-do attitude is the true spirit of punk rock. Ryan should have recognized that beneath Mac's AstroTurfed exterior was a thumping punk heart. But it wasn't just Ryan; I didn't recognize it, either. None of us could get past the shitty PA and the sports posters on the walls. Looking back on it, Whiskeytown should have shut up and made do, workmanlike, without complaint, four-channel PA and all.

I eventually got the equipment loaded into the trailer and the people loaded into the van. I climbed behind the wheel, and we fishtailed out of there, leaving Jenni to settle up with Norm and Kenny. Driving away, I felt horrible for her. Whiskeytown had just shit all over her homecoming. She would later say it was the most humiliating night of her life.

Ryan had made the classic mistake of punishing the fans who *were* focused on the band by lashing out at the people who *weren't* paying attention. He'd eventually use my computer to go online and type up a drunken apology: *I am truly sorry you have to endure how i feel, just to get the music I make,* he wrote. *But after all, thats what you paid for isnt it.*

Ryan would hold a grudge against East Lansing for years. Later, we'd print up a Whiskeytown concert shirt that had tour dates listed on the back. *Boston, New York, East Lansing,* it read. *Philadelphia, DC, East Lansing. Atlanta, Tampa, East Lansing. Los Angeles, San Diego, East Lansing.*

CHAPTER

A few weeks after the East Lansing debacle, the big coast-to-coast *Strangers Almanac* tour kicked off with an album release show at the Brewery in Raleigh. This was the huge hometown gig. Sold out. Saturday night. Summertime in the Southland. The sidewalk that ran along Hillsborough Street, past the Brewery and the adjacent Comet Lounge, was lined with people smoking cigarettes and wearing pearl-buttoned cowboy shirts, waiting for the doors to open. Whiskeytown's major-label debut was now officially out and standing tall in the CD bins of record stores nationwide. The days of *soon-to-be* and *forthcoming* were over. Now it was time for Ryan and the band to deliver on all that promise and potential.

As the crowd filed in, I stood at the side of the stage, working to keep the guitars in tune. Earlier that day we'd done an acoustic in-store in a Chapel Hill record shop. Now we were about to put on the real show, the one that mattered. And because the record was out, everything seemed to matter more. I felt a hollow space in the pit of my stomach. And I wasn't even in the band.

I raised my head from the tuner and looked around the Brewery, thinking that it had barely changed since 1986, when I first was here with ANTiSEEN. Capacity of about three hundred, all standing, no seats. Smelling of spilled beer and cigarette smoke. Stage offset in the corner with a few lights hanging overhead. The PA was nothing special, but in-house soundman Jac Cain always had the room sounding better than it should have. In the nearly fifteen years since it opened, the Brewery had become Raleigh's go-to place to catch touring acts on the way up. Black Flag, the Descendants, Jane's Addiction, Soul Asylum, and just about every punk and alternative band that came through the Triangle from the mideighties to the midnineties had played here. The typical Brewery crowd was a mixed bag. Punk rats. Metal dudes. Flannel-clad alterna-chicks. Because it sat right on Hillsborough, just west of NC State, on some nights it felt like campus property. You'd have sorority girls sitting at the bar, splitting a pitcher of cheap draft; maybe there'd be some John Edwards-looking fratboy snorting coke in the bathroom. Other nights it would be filled with thirtysomethings who'd arranged for a babysitter so they could check out a show by a local veteran like Don Dixon.

The Brewery would eventually be shuttered and bulldozed in 2011, succumbing to the rising rents and gentrification patterns that claimed renowned music venues across America, from CBGB in New York to the Uptown in Minneapolis to Liberty Lunch in Austin. Today, on the block where the Brewery and the Comet once stood, you'll find high-rise, ultraluxe student apartments: *catch some rays while floating on a raft in our oasis saltwater pool . . . we have it all (and more)!* At street level, instead of a smoky, boozy rock club, you'll find a store selling *Smoothies with a Purpose* to coeds in fifty-dollar yoga pants.

Up and down Hillsborough Street, many of the old dives and mom-and-pops are now gone, replaced by corporate-clean storefronts that offer the current generation of NC State students (and their protective parents) the familiar comfort of upscale national chains. On the east end of the strip, at the spot where Sadlack's Heroes and Schoolkids Records once stood, you'll now find an Aloft Hotel, the striving-for-hip franchise whose WXYZ hotel bar claims to be "an eclectic space that's always thriving with live DJs and emerging artists." Nice try, but the Aloft will never be half as eclectic as the old haunts that were razed to clear space for it.

On the night of the *Strangers Almanac* release show, Hillsborough Street was still Hillsborough Street, which means that the Brewery was choked with Marlboro smoke and the beer taps were running wide. Same story next door at the Comet, where lots of people hung out before and after Brewery shows. As I watched the room fill up, I knew the audience that night would mostly be the forgiving type: superfans happy to eat whatever the band cooked up. But there would also be a few bitter scenesters, half-hoping for Ryan and the band to fail, hate-watching the whole time, maybe sticking around for a song or three and then retreating to the Comet to talk shit about how overrated Whiskeytown is.

That sort of jealous backlash comes part and parcel with any thriving music scene, and it would be hard to overstate just how thriving the Raleigh-Durham-Chapel Hill scene was in the mid-nineties. By 1997, having a local band celebrate a national record release had become routine. Like a lot of musical hotbeds, the Triangle was blessed with the trifecta of being a good-sized metro area that boasted the state capital and also contained the campus of a major university—in our case, *three* of them: North Carolina State, the University of North Carolina, and Duke. Austin, Minneapolis-St. Paul, Nashville, Columbus, and Madison all share this combination of sizable population, state government, and higher education, and in their own way all of them had become significant locales on the musical map.

But for an area of its size, the Triangle had *way* more than its share of prominent bands and record labels. That summer of 1997, the Raleigh-Durham-Chapel Hill metropolitan area had a population of 1,050,054, which made it only the 43rd largest metro area in the country, smaller than Rochester (40th), Memphis (41st), and Jacksonville (42nd). However, thanks to the economic migration that brought people from the Rust Belt down to the New South, the Triangle was the 14th *fastest-growing* metro area in America. Ever since the late 1980s, its musical landscape had been booming in tandem with its population. Metal band Corrosion of Conformity signed with Columbia. Later, so did Southern rockers Cry of Love. The Connells signed to TVT Records. Ben Folds Five went to Sony. Mercury Records swept up the Veldt. My guys Lustre signed with A&M. Archers of Loaf were on Alias Records. Chapel Hill's Superchunk were becoming indie rock legends, and their label, Merge Records— in addition to picking up local bands like Polvo—was on a roll that would eventually have them sign acts as prominent as Arcade Fire, Spoon, and Bob Mould. The town next door, Carrboro, was home to Mammoth Records, which got its start by releasing albums from out-of-towners like Tucson's the Sidewinders, Boston's Blake Babies, New Orleans's Dash Rip Rock, and, later, Orlando's aforementioned Seven Mary Three. But recently Mammoth had set its sights locally, signing Triangle acts Dillon Fence and the Squirrel Nut Zippers, the neoswing combo whose 1996 album *Hot* gave Mammoth—and the Triangle—a platinum seller.

Local up-and-comers the Backsliders were also signed to Mammoth, and they were near the center of the Triangle's newly exploding alt-country scene, of which Whiskeytown was currently the leading light. But there was also Southern Culture on the Skids, who'd been picked up by Geffen. And Flat Duo Jets, who took rockabilly out of the country and into the garage. Plus 6 String Drag, who would record for Steve Earle's E-Squared label. And Jolene, who would sign with Sire. To some extent, all these alt-country acts were following a trail blazed by legendary local Terry Anderson, who'd written "Battleship Chains," a song that the Georgia Satellites covered on their 1986 debut and that the Hindu Love Gods (Warren Zevon plus all the members of R.E.M. except for Michael Stipe) put on their eponymous 1990 release. The very week of the Brewery show, the *News & Observer* called the Triangle "ground zero for insurgent country." *No Depression* magazine had also labeled North Carolina the home base of alt-country, and its cofounder, Peter Blackstock, was so taken by the area, he'd later *move* here.

Now at the Brewery, as I got the stage ready for the show, the whole dynamic felt like a series of Russian nesting dolls: Raleigh's alt-country scene was booming inside of the larger music scene that was booming inside of the Raleigh-Durham-Chapel Hill metro area that was booming inside of the booming New South. Who gave a good-goddamn about being the next Seattle? We were the first motherfucking Triangle. And Whiskeytown was the right band, at the right place, at the right time.

Better yet, in *Strangers Almanac* they had the right album, one that had the potential to transcend alt-country and push Ryan and

Whiskeytown right into the mainstream. One review after another mentioned that Whiskeytown and *Strangers Almanac* were poised to trade alt-country's core fanbase for a widespread audience. *USA Today* noted that country was merely the starting point for the record, that "the hillbilly element was rivaled by the music's rock energy, pop smarts, and Adams's unselfconsciously literate writing." *Rolling Stone*'s three-star review (written by Grant Alden, who coedited *No Depression* along with Blackstock) read, "If there's to be a Nirvana among the bands that are imprecisely dubbed alt-country, look to Whiskeytown."

A review in the *Austin American-Statesman* began with a reminder that for all its buzz, alt-country still hadn't made much of a dent in the marketplace: "To go by Soundscan sales figures, the existence of an alternative country movement is still just a rumor yet to be confirmed." The article suggested, however, that Whiskeytown "might just change all that." And the reason that they more than other alt-country acts might find commercial success was their *accessibility*, "embodied by the melodic gifts of twenty-two-year-old Ryan Adams." In Ryan you didn't necessarily hear the country influence of Johnny Cash or Merle Haggard or Buck Owens; instead, you heard "traces of early Jackson Browne, which is not a bad place to be musically, especially if you want to sell records." The *American-Statesman* argued furthermore that unlike other country-rock artists, Ryan's voice was an easier listen for the mainstream, "a sound that can appeal to a wider audience." The common thread among these reviews was that Ryan's smart lyrics and pop melodies, when delivered via his pleasing voice, made *Strangers Almanac* palatable to listeners who weren't sold on acts that served up more grit, gravel, and twang.

However, within alt-country circles, *accessibility* was potentially a negative. When any form of art—be it alt-country, punk rock, slam poetry, or graffiti—threatens to expand from its niche origins and become commercially successful (which is to say, when that art form moves from *folk* to *mass*), the popular manifestations of the art are often considered less pure than the versions that *didn't* catch on. And the criticism can be especially fierce when coming from inside the original niche community itself. I could imagine the backlash from all the alt-country bands that had not been signed and were fed up with reading about Whiskeytown's major-label success, telling themselves that Ryan had *watered it down*, while they, still toiling in obscurity, were *keeping it real*. Ryan, angling for mainstream radio play, was a *poseur*, but these guys, playing mandolins and banjos for their *No Depression* buddies on Tuesday nights, were *credible*.

Strangers Almanac was accessible, no doubt, which, as the *Austin Chronicle* pointed out, left "Whiskeytown open to charges that they sold out just in time for their major label debut." In making such a slick, accessible record, had Whiskeytown sacrificed authenticity? Moreover, had Ryan Adams ever been "authentic" in the first place? And how do you define "authentic" anyway?

This question of whether or not Ryan was "real" or just an extremely talented faker had been dogging him since Whiskeytown's inception. In the song "Faithless Street," he sings, *So I started this damn country band / Cause punk rock was too hard to sing*. In the two years since the release of the *Faithless Street* album, music writers had gravitated toward that line—maybe because it seemed to contain a naked admission from Ryan that his move from punk to country was calculated rather than authentic.

As the *Boston Phoenix* put it in a profile of Whiskeytown, "authenticity can be measured in different ways. Does an artist who sings about hard times and unemployment have had to have grown up in a tarpaper shack in Mississippi in order to be authentic?"

I'd answer, hell no. But Ryan really did grow up in a small Southern city. He'd earned the right to sing about small towns, dive bars, and run-down motels just as much as anybody. And yet, as *Strangers Almanac* hit stores, he anticipated that the "Ryan-isn't-real" critique might intensify. "I think, because of my age," he told the *News & Observer*, "some people will think this record is a smart kid just making stuff up."

Outpost Recordings' Mark Williams also heard the criticism: "People aren't really listening if they take Ryan to task for not being 'real,'" he said. "I don't think you can get much realer in terms of being true to yourself and writing straight from the heart. The guy is the closest thing to a pure songwriter I've ever come across." Given that Williams had been an early champion of R.E.M. and through the course of his thirty-plus-year career as a record executive would work with Cracker, Smashing Pumpkins, Beck, the Hives, Pharrell Williams, and Jack White, this is a guy who came across a lot of songwriters.

Ryan Adams created a country-punk-meets-Paul-Westerberg persona for himself. And along with Caitlin, he created the fiddle-and-acoustic-heavy sound of Whiskeytown. Were this image and sound contrived? Maybe. But one person's contrivance is another person's vision. Every great artist is contrived to some degree. Dylan and Springsteen are both contrived. They're playing characters of their own creation. But they also had a vision for how to execute the contrivance, and they executed it so well, we bought it.

Compare Springsteen to Bon Jovi. The conventional wisdom is that Bruce is the real authentic deal and Bon Jovi is the fake. But maybe that just means that Springsteen is a better actor, which is to say, when he plays the "Springsteen" character, it doesn't look to us like acting, so we believe him. With Bon Jovi, on the other hand, we see the wires. We sense the man behind the curtain, pulling the levers. Authenticity is in the eye of the beholder. Everybody's faking it. "Visionary" is what we call artists who don't look like they're faking. As I once told the journalist David Menconi, Ryan really did do the drugs and drink the liquor and write the songs. And a lot of that was done specifically to build up the "Ryan Adams" character. Ryan knew exactly what he was doing, and his persona was absolutely calculated. But unlike Bon Jovi and so many others, Ryan's character was *well* calculated.

Even as a teenager, Ryan was keenly aware of the importance of looking and sounding authentic. In his book about Whiskeytown, *Ryan Adams: Losering*, Menconi recounts a scene of an eighteen-year-old Ryan practicing with Lazy Stars, a short-lived band he formed not long after moving to Raleigh. As can be heard on a bootleg recording, after playing a song called "Withering Heights," Ryan asks bandmate Tom Cushman if he can understand what he is singing. "Not really," Tom says. After a pause, Ryan says, "Do I sound like I mean it?"

Ryan understood that you don't have to mean it. But you have to *sound* like you do. And listeners have to believe you. When they do, that *makes* you authentic. And from the minute Ryan arrived in Raleigh, there were those in town who didn't believe him, those who thought he was heavy on ambition but light on authenticity. Then again, there were also plenty of folks who fell for young Ryan hard and fast, and many of those people were music writers, club owners, and record label reps—the very kind of devotees you need if you hope to build a career.

Outpost's Mark Williams was the one who recommended that Jim Scott—who had recorded Tom Petty's *Wildflowers*—produce *Strangers Almanac*. In an effort to gauge Scott's interest in Whiskeytown, Williams sent the producer a tape of the demos.

According to Williams, Scott "immediately reacted to the songwriting and to Ryan's voice. His catch phrase was 'I believe him.'" Ryan told *No Depression*'s Peter Blackstock that later, once they were in the studio working on the vocals, Scott "would listen to a couple takes, and he'd say, 'I believe this guy.' That's how he would talk about it. He wouldn't ever put it on me; he'd listen to the recording and go, 'This is the guy I believe.'"

Scott was reacting to the authenticity, not of Ryan the man, but of the persona Ryan was adopting for each individual song, a persona that can be put on or taken off at will. As Sir Laurence Olivier allegedly said to Dustin Hoffman after the younger actor had stayed awake for three days straight in order to appear authentically exhausted in a scene from *Marathon Man*, "My dear boy, have you tried *acting?*" Ryan Adams had tried acting, and he was a natural.

Judging by the critical reaction to *Strangers Almanac*, Whiskeytown had established that accessibility and authenticity didn't have to be mutually exclusive, that listeners could not only like Ryan and his palatable voice—they could also *believe* it. A review in the *Houston Chronicle* sure seemed to buy it: "The so-called alternative country movement has [. . .] been too sprawling, too lazy, and too self-aware to make many waves commensurate with the hype it generates. Whiskeytown succeeds where others have failed simply by offering a much more consistent and committed effort. This band sounds like it means it."

Here at The Brewery, Whiskeytown took the stage, and the crowd went nuts. Out in the audience, on the other side of the fourth wall, it was instantly obvious that this was a special show: the formal send-off for the local heroes who were all set up to conquer the world.

But onstage, it felt like no big deal, like just another gig in Cleveland or Birmingham. Ryan wasn't superdrunk and irritated like he'd been at Mac's Bar; he just seemed bored. And the band was sloppy. Maybe they'd downed a few too many preshow beers to calm the nerves. Or maybe the additional slop was because in the month since East Lansing, a new musician had joined the band—multi-instrumentalist Mike Daly—and with the addition of a sixth member, the group hadn't quite jelled.

Jim Scott's production on *Strangers Almanac* was slick and lush—not at all raw, rootsy, and lo-fi. It didn't sound like it had been taped live in a honky-tonk; it sounded like it had been crafted in expensive studios in Nashville and Los Angeles, which it had been. And because the recordings featured instrumentation—mandolin, lapsteel, keys—that was beyond what the band typically employed in a live set, Ryan and his managers at Jacknife had been trying to find a musician who could add those bonus ingredients on the road.

This was 1997, fifteen years before seemingly every hipster had grown a beard, learned to play mandolin, and dreamed of auditioning for the Avett Brothers or Mumford & Sons. Back then there wasn't a surplus of skinny-jeaned, suspender-wearing lumber-dudes playing lapsteel and banjo. Today, obviously, that has changed. You can go to any college town in America and find a dozen copies of that person. But in the nineties, if you were looking for somebody who played all those bluegrass instruments, you pretty much had to head into the hollers of Kentucky or West Virginia and dig up a washtub band. Or you could go to Nashville and find one of those seventy-year-old session cats who totally ripped on pedal steel. But that type of guy wasn't about to hop into a van and tour the country with a bunch of drunken punks. The only other cool-looking, mandolin-playing multi-instrumentalist any of us had heard of was

Waiting to Derail

Peter Holsapple from iconic Winston-Salem band the dB's, but he was already moonlighting with R.E.M. and Hootie & the Blowfish. So, as Whiskeytown was about to set off on the *Strangers Almanac* tour, tracking down a utility person with the right look and musical chops was like unicorn hunting.

But Jacknife was able to unearth Mike Daly. A Jersey guy, he had studied at the Berklee College of Music and then played in a band called Swales. He was a whiz on pedal steel, lapsteel, organ, piano, and mandolin, and he was a great guitar player. Like everybody else in Whiskeytown, Mike Daly was young, but the dude was a pro, more composed than anybody in our touring party, me included. And maybe it was the quick hit of his four-letter first and last names, but for some reason we always called him "Mike Daly," never just "Mike" or "Daly."

Mike Daly's debut appearance in the lineup happened in the weeks between East Lansing and the Brewery. It was at Tramps in Manhattan, opening for Cracker. As far as I know, the first time anybody in the band met him was that afternoon at sound check. Even without a proper practice, he was able to sit in on a few songs—during a high-pressure NYC show in front of the Outpost-Geffen label people, no less—and pull it off admirably.

After the Tramps gig, Mike Daly hauled a small music store's worth of gear down to Raleigh, where the plan was for him to rehearse with the band all week before taking the stage at the Brewery and then continuing as the sixth Whiskeytowner for the ensuing national tour. Like I said, Mike Daly is a pro, so by the time he crossed the Mason-Dixon, he knew *Strangers Almanac* backward and forward, but he still wanted to get in some meaningful practice time. The guy was juggling guitar, keys, and lapsteel; he was looking for feedback from Ryan about which instrument to play in which song. So a week

[50]

before the Brewery show, he checked in to a Days Inn in a desolate part of Raleigh and waited for Ryan or Phil or somebody to call him about practice.

The band may have rehearsed with Mike Daly once. Mostly he spent that week holed up in his room with his instruments, playing along to the record, singlehandedly making all the orchestration decisions. "It's *your* fucking jobs to learn these songs," Phil told him during one of the few times they spoke that week. "We already know them. It's not our job to teach them to you."

I'm sure Caitlin would have loved to rehearse with Mike Daly every day, but she'd get overruled by Ryan and Phil and their desire not to let band practice to get in the way of whatever else it was they were doing, which was probably sleeping until 4:00 p.m. and then rolling straight from bed to happy hour.

The Brewery show would kick off the first bona fide national tour, where Whiskeytown would be supported by radio play and record reviews and the full faith and credit of a major-label machine. And instead of rehearsing with their new utility player, the band had spent the week leading up to the show dicking around.

Now, up on stage, the lack of practice was showing. Everyone individually was fine, but as a unit they were nowhere near as tight as they could have been. And there was no effort on anybody's part to make the hometown show feel distinct. No sweeteners for the local faithful. This was a Vegas set: short, generic, and uninspired. It was okay. But it was *just* okay. And *just okay* is no way to celebrate the release of a major-label debut. The band yawned through the songs and then, without much fanfare, walked off the stage.

By the end, even the crowd seemed anxious to get the show over with so that the serious drinking could commence. People were standing around, sipping beers, maybe mumbling for an encore but certainly not chanting in unison for one more song. From my spot on the side of the stage, it looked like the band members had disappeared. Some were probably mingling in the crowd. Ryan was probably next door at the Comet, ordering up a nightcap or asking around for a dose of stiffer medication. The show hadn't ended so much as fizzled out.

Getting ready to pack up the gear, I was confused, bordering on irate. Ryan's band was all set up on the major-label launchpad, and the kid seemed content to botch the whole thing before achieving liftoff. I was sad for him and for me. Maybe I'd made a huge mistake taking this gig. My career might be the collateral damage wrought by Ryan's implosion.

Then he walked back onstage, all by himself, and started digging through a rat's nest of instrument cables and toppled beer bottles. The crowd hadn't quite noticed him. He didn't look like he was coming back for an encore; he looked like a teenager trying to find a lost sock on the floor of a messy bedroom. But then he picked up his Guild acoustic, plugged in, strummed a quick chord. The audience noise swelled a bit, but mostly people were still drinking and talking, not really watching him. He stood alone, picking that guitar, now finding rhythm but still half-drowned out by the murmur of bar talk. Then he leaned into the mic and began to sing about which direction the taxi cabs run and how they can't make it to where his love interest lives.

A few people cheered, recognizing the song, but most just fell quiet, and by the time Ryan sang a line about lying in his lover's arms, the crowd was nearly silent, everybody staring rapt at the stage. Twenty seconds earlier, the audience was yammering and bottles were clanking. Now everyone had stopped what they were doing and turned toward the kid standing alone with his guitar. The Brewery was so quiet you could almost hear the sole of a Converse All-Star squeaking on the floor. The song, which is called "Avenues," was so beautiful, and the way it had hushed the crowd was so powerful, I was mesmerized just like everybody else.

"Avenues" is the tenth track on *Strangers Almanac*, but hearing it that night was like hearing it for the first time. I'd certainly never heard it played that poignantly. In the two months I had been with the band, I'd never seen Ryan play solo acoustic like this. I hadn't had a chance to spend any time with the album, either. As soon as you get a tour-managing job, you instantly have a million things to do: advance the shows, book the hotels, rent the van and trailer. I hadn't had time to sit down and give the record a good listen.

But I was listening now. And I was fucking stunned by what I was hearing: Ryan singing about the world's sweethearts and how they're dancing in the very same places where he and all his buddies go to hide their faces. The words—self-deprecating and vulnerable, spilling from the mouth of a kid who just a few weeks before was telling all of East Lansing to go fuck itself—were a breathtaking contradiction to the behavior. To this day, Ryan performing "Avenues" by himself at the Brewery, on a stage littered with beer bottles and toppled cymbal stands, is one of the most memorable experiences of my career. I imagine it was like seeing Dylan at Café Wha? or Springsteen at the Bitter End.

Over the course of two minutes and thirty-one seconds, I went from *Oh, well, I'm working with this guy that's probably going to piss away both of our careers* to *Holy shit, Ryan Adams is a fucking genius. I get it. This guy is the absolute real deal. Authentic as anybody.*

[53]

Ryan wasn't the next Jay Farrar or Jeff Tweedy or Rhett Miller or whoever the current alt-country darling was. He was better. He was on another plane altogether, up there with Springsteen, Neil Young, Tom Petty, and, yes, Dylan. Not just talented, but special. No, more than special: important. Before he ended the song, I could see that Ryan's career as a singer/songwriter was going to last just as long as he wanted it to last.

Ryan finished up and then put down his guitar to the most sincere applause I'd heard all night. Whiskeytown played one more song as a whole band, and then the show was over.

As I was packing the gear, Ryan walked up to me. "How was that?" he said.

"Man," I said. "That 'Avenues' song needs to be the first encore every night."

He mulled that idea over for a second. "Okay," he said. And then he disappeared into the Comet Lounge.

As he walked away, I was absolutely certain that Ryan Adams was bound for greatness—if he could keep from self-destructing. Two avenues running in opposite directions. I left the bar that night wondering which route he was going to take.

CHAPTER

The Atlanta show was long over, and upstairs at Smith's Olde Bar, the crowd had gathered their belongings and gone home. The bar-back was pushing a broom across the floor. The bartender was wiping down the counter with a rag. The band—most of them, anyway—had all scattered. Some were nursing Budweisers in the restaurant downstairs; some were wandering up Piedmont and Monroe, looking for pay phones, liquor stores, the piney-fresh air of the night. But Steven Terry, the drummer, was still sitting at the bar, hitting on a chick he'd met earlier.

I had already settled up with the club, and now I was just trying to get the gear down the long staircase and out of there. This wasn't an arena tour; we were playing clubs. We only had two people on the crew—Bruce Neese and me—so each band member was responsible for packing up their own equipment. All the guitars and amps were loaded. The cables were wound and stowed. Everybody else had done their job. But there on the stage was Steven's drum set, still pristinely assembled, untouched in the last hour. And there at the bar, ass glued to a stool, was the drummer himself. Instead of packing up his kit, he was playing postshow rock star.

So I walked up to him, and I stood there, meaning to be polite, not wanting to interrupt him or throw him off his game. I stood there. And I stood there. And I was obviously standing there because I needed something from him. But he didn't acknowledge me. The guy was laying the BS down thick.

"That's how it is," he said to the girl. "We roll into a different town every day. We pour our heart and soul into the show." He paused to take a sip from his beer. "And when it's over," he slowly shook his head, "we've got nothing left."

Sweet Christ. The "that's how it is on the road" speech. I'd heard enough. "Okay, Bon Jovi," I said, cupping him on the shoulder. "How 'bout you pack up your drums and we get the fuck out of here."

It was the second night of the tour.

A few days earlier, I'd gone to the Cruise America location in Cary, North Carolina, and rented an RV. A Jamboree Searcher by Fleetwood, with the nose of a van and the ass of a camper. I drove. Bruce, the soundman, rode shotgun. Above our heads was a loft, perfect for a 65-mph nap. Behind us was an efficiency kitchen with a minifridge and propane stove. Also, a working and well-used bathroom. In the way back: a bedroom. No trailer this time, as having an extra thousand pounds dragging off the tail would make for tough maneuvering, especially on a tour that would take us over the Rockies and out to the West Coast. So we loaded all the gear through the side door and into the back bedroom. We stashed the smaller cases in the RV's many strategically placed storage cubbies.

Leaving Raleigh that August of 1997, we were a party of eight: Bruce, me, and six Whiskeytowners: Ryan, Caitlin, Phil, Steven, Chris, and Mike Daly. The tour started with a run through the Southeast: Columbia, Atlanta, Birmingham. Less than a week in, everybody was tired and irritated. The band was tired from the heroic quantities of alcohol they were throwing down, and I was irritated from the effort it took every night to get their drunken asses out of the bar and every morning to get their hungover asses out of the hotel, into the RV, and off to the next town. Ryan and Phil spent most of the miles bickering at each other. Caitlin may have been like Ryan's sensible big sister, but Phil was Ryan's "fuck it" brother. The two guitar players were constantly sniping, constantly trying to one-up each other, onstage and off. On those long drives, Phil, in the older brother role, would give Ryan grief about anything and everything: his hair, his clothes, his taste in music.

"Fuck you," Ryan would say.

"No, fuck you," Phil would answer. "You pussy."

"I'm tired of your shit," Ryan would pout.

Mike Daly, the consummate professional, would never chime in, but Chris Laney and Steven Terry sure would.

Meanwhile, Caitlin would be trying to concentrate on a book. "Shut up, you guys," she'd say. "Quit it." I felt sorry for her, trapped in an RV with these squabbling idiots.

After Birmingham, heading north on I-95 on the way to New York, we passed a sign that read RALEIGH 35, and I thought, *Please, can't I just go home?* This job was much tougher than escorting Lustre or D Generation across the country, and for a minute I seriously considered taking a hard left at Benson and rolling on back to Raleigh.

But I kept the wheel straight, and we made it to Manhattan for an important show at the Mercury Lounge. Playing New York is always a big deal, but for a new band touring behind a major-label debut, the stakes in NYC are especially high. Huge labels have access to huge promotional resources, but they can't put every bit of those resources behind every one of their bands. All the acts on the roster are competing for a slice of a limited (albeit massive) promotional pie. One way a band might be treated to a fatter hunk of that pie is to impress the product managers, radio promoters, and field-marketing reps that come out to the shows, and more of them show up in New York and Los Angeles than, say, at your average Tuesday night in Shreveport.

The Mercury Lounge show was in fact on a Tuesday, which is inconvenient for most civilians but just fine for label reps for whom going to see bands is a regular part of the work week. Whiskeytown's single, "16 Days," was just starting to make waves at alternative and Americana radio stations. The New York gig was a chance to remind the Outpost staff—and the execs at Outpost's parent companies, Geffen Records and Universal Music Group—why they'd been so fired up about Ryan in the first place.

For his part, Ryan didn't care about impressing company types. He was excited because New York was where his new girlfriend, Amy, lived. Ryan had met Amy when she was Debbie-Southwood-Smith's assistant. Now she was working at Warner Bros. Records, and "Avenues," the song that had blown me away at the *Strangers Almanac* release show, was apparently written about her. Ryan was doubly psyched because his attorney was supposed to bring another one of his clients out to the show: Bob Mould, the legendary frontman from Hüsker Dü and Sugar.

Despite all the pressure on account of who was in the crowd—suits, girlfriend, punk rock luminary—Whiskeytown didn't disappoint that night. They were solid. Great songs played well.

Simple as that. A review of the show in *Rolling Stone* read: ". . . the twangy, Raleigh, NC, sextet earnestly and passionately evoked the rich traditions of country music . . . [with] enough barreling electric guitar to keep an adoring urban crown shouting out requests." Better still, before the show, out on the sidewalk in front of the club, Ryan and I got to meet Bob Mould. During the conversation, Ryan pointed out that I'd been in ANTiSEEN. Bob mentioned that he'd seen us, and he asked if ANTiSEEN singer Jeff Clayton was still *juicing* (which was the old pro wrestling trick of making tiny cuts in your forehead before a match so that come showtime you would bleed easier—the answer was *yes*). Bob was a loyal pro wrestling fan, and a couple years after we met him on Houston Street, he would take a job writing scripts for WCW. Most important, that night Ryan and Bob kindled a friendship that has lasted for two decades.

But there was no time to revel in the Big Apple triumph. Northampton, Massachusetts, awaited. By then, Ryan's guitar strap stunk so bad from sweat and mold that it had become a biohazard-grade threat to the RV's air quality. We had to powerwash it with a hose and let it disinfect in the sun. Then we were on to Boston for a show at Bill's Bar, which was on Lansdowne Street, right across from Fenway. The Red Sox had played a game that night, and although the home team beat the Twins, 6–1, the crowd was salty. Even with the win, the Sox were sitting at four games below .500 and fourth place in the AL East. Plus at that point they hadn't won the World Series in seventy-nine years, the Celtics had sucked since 1988, and Tom Brady had yet to arrive in New England, so yeah: Boston sports fans were salty, all right. They brought their Fenway heckling across the street to Bill's. During one of the band's extended song breaks, some guy yelled toward the stage, "You bunch of rookies!" I looked at Ryan and braced for a sequel to the East Lansing fiasco, but this time he kept his Earnhardt-won-the-Super-Bowl-by-hitting-a-home-run mockery of sports in check.

Next we zigged down to Philly and Arlington, Virginia, and then we zagged back up to Toronto. The tension between Ryan and Phil was escalating. It had gone beyond put-downs and taunts and had started to get physical, the two of them exchanging elbows, then punches on the arm, then headlocks and half nelsons. At one point Caitlin, while trying to break up Ryan and Phil, accidentally got hit. She was pissed—the way a big sister gets pissed at her dumb-ass younger brothers. I started to feel less like a tour manager and more like a referee for Whiskeytown Championship Wrestling. While keeping the RV between the white lines, I also needed to keep the peace.

Thanks to the dirty laundry and the smell of cigarette smoke (some of it emanating not just from the clothes but from the *gear*), the RV was no longer, shall we say, showroom fresh. One of the curtain rods was hanging limp. Somebody had taken a Sharpie to the back exterior of the camper, and underneath the spot where it read FLEETWOOD, that clever genius had scrawled MAC. I wondered how much of the rental deposit that bit of comedy gold would eat up.

After Toronto, we crossed back into the United States via the Ambassador Bridge, which connects Windsor to Detroit. I later learned that the Ambassador Bridge serves as the training site for all agents who work the US/Canada border, so this checkpoint was extra-thorough. Totally by the book. Most bands avoid it by crossing at Point Edward, sixty miles to the north.

The customs agent, a six-foot-something, mustached Michigander, looked me over and then stuck his big head through the window, scanning toward the back of the RV where the six Whiskeytowners were slouching. "Everybody get out," he said.

I explained that we were a band, and I was the tour manager. I told him I appreciated that he was doing his job, but he was wasting his time. "Look," I said. "We're not stupid enough to bring drugs through a border crossing."

"You might be their tour manager," he said, "but you're not their mama." Then he turned to his female partner, and giving the RV a little love tap, he smiled and said, "Needle in a haystack."

They started tearing the camper apart, going through our bags, the storage cubbies, the equipment cases. After a while, they dug up a stash of books: Steinbeck paperbacks that Caitlin and Chris Laney were sharing.

"Aww, man," the big agent said, smiling wide and holding a copy of *Cannery Row*. "I love Steinbeck. He's one of my favorites." In fact, he told us, *Tortilla Flat* was sitting on his nightstand at that moment.

The customs agent, Caitlin, and Chris proceeded to have a discussion about Steinbeck's place in the American literary canon. An impromptu meeting of the Ambassador Bridge Book Club: all diesel exhaust, no Pinot Grigio.

The border search was instantly over. They waved us straight on through. As we drove around downtown Detroit looking for the on-ramp to I-75, Steven Terry unscrewed a giant canister of protein powder. "Fuck, man," he said. "That was close." He pulled a bag of weed from the canister and held it up for us to inspect.

Around noon the next day, we left Pontiac, Michigan, aiming for Chicago. Phil had caught a car ride with a friend, so the RV was a man down. Even though he and Ryan constantly argued, and even though they had a habit of double-dog-daring each other into getting more and more wasted and doing dumber and dumber shit, Phil, I'd come to learn, could be something of a stabilizing influence on Ryan. Even in their mutual drunkenness, Phil could kowtow Ryan into being moderately responsible—emphasis on *moderately*, which is to say not responsible at all compared to most adult Americans.

He was the pressure valve. He helped spread the jackassery out over two people. When Phil was gone, like now on the drive to Chicago, Ryan felt the full heat of the spotlight, and he would drink for two, smoke for two, be jackass enough for two. With Phil out of the way, it was quieter in the RV, and there was less bickering. But less bickering meant more drinking. Ryan spent the whole ride west on I-94 with a bottle of Beam between his legs. By the time we got to Chicago, he was so hammered he kept staring, catatonic, out the window at Lake Michigan, saying, "Wow, look at the Gulf of Mexico."

It was Friday night in the City of the Big Shoulders, and this was a really big show. If Raleigh was the headquarters of alt-country, Chicago was the northern branch office, home of Bloodshot Records, which would become one of the two or three most significant Americana labels. Whiskeytown was currently the alt-country band riding the tallest wave, so Ryan was shouldering the weight of the whole movement, like it or not. But as we loaded into the Double Door for sound check, Ryan was so drunk he could barely stand up— undone by the hundred-and-a-half pounds of his own body.

We met up with Phil, fumbled through sound check, and then Ryan was scheduled to do an interview with Mark Gaurino from the *Chicago Daily Herald*, the newspaper of suburban Chicagoland. Gaurino walked with Ryan to a liquor store and then down Milwaukee

Avenue to Nick's Beer Garden, where Ryan got even more sauced on Budweiser and Jagermeister. "I'm tired, I'm drunk, I haven't had any sleep," Ryan told Gaurino. "Look at me. I'm damaged. I'm twenty-two years old and I look forty." The interview ended with Ryan splayed on the sidewalk somewhere between Nick's and the Double Door.

Showtime was in about an hour, and it was taking every bit of Ryan's coordination just to stay upright. No way was he going to be able to play guitar and sing. So Phil and I took charge. We helped Ryan get to the RV, where he promptly passed out. Then I went down the street to a Mexican joint, where I bought him a burrito and a Pepsi. Back in the RV, Phil whipped out two packets of Goody's Powder. An ingenious mix of aspirin, acetaminophen, and caffeine, Goody's was the South's go-to hangover cure (mind you, I'm a tour manager, not a doctor—combine Goody's with alcohol at your own risk). I was impressed that Phil was so quick to come to his fallen comrade's aid. It was kind of sweet: they were the two guys on the record contract, and they'd become the type of brothers that constantly messed with each other, but if one of them was being messed with by somebody else, then they had each other's back. Phil tore open the packets and poured them into Ryan's Pepsi.

"Drink this, you pussy," he said. Brotherly sweetness only went so far.

Ryan was miserable. He could barely find the strength and coordination to spit out a fuck you. But the food and caffeine helped, and he eventually gained his footing—enough to make it a few steps into the bathroom. I could hear him first gagging, then retching, then yelling, "I'm dying in here!"

Phil just laughed.

"Fuck you, dude," Ryan said. "I'm dying."

I opened the door and found him hunched over the toilet. "Look," he said. "I'm throwing up blood. There's blood everywhere."

Shit. Maybe the double dose of Goody's had triggered stomach bleeding. I peeked into the bowl, which was indeed red. A split second of real panic. Then, looking at the contents of the bowl, I started laughing.

Ryan wiped his mouth with his sleeve. "What?" he said.

"Dude, that's not blood," I said. "You puked up half a burrito. That's *salsa*."

The Double Door was packed. And that, the size of the audience, was the gig's only highlight. Ryan could barely speak, much less carry a show. This was the worst Whiskeytown performance I'd seen so far, by far. A review in the *Chicago Sun-Times* ran under the headline: *A 'loaded' singer dilutes Whiskeytown's promise.* "What does an emerging band owe its fans?" the article began. "Apparently nothing." The critic called the band "uninspired and sloppy," saying that "Whiskeytown gave one of this year's most disappointing shows . . ."

But Saturday's newspaper is Sunday's fishwrapper. And by the time the *Sun-Times* review hit Chicago's newsstands, the RV was four-hundred miles south, and we were long past caring. Instead, it was a different account of the show that ended up sticking with us, a profile written by Mark Gaurino, the writer who'd gone with Ryan to the liquor store and the beer garden. Gaurino seemed to be a fan of Replacements, so when his story of the night described Whiskeytown as "loose" and as a band that "rocks full out," he meant *loose* as a compliment. In Gaurino's piece, Ryan doesn't read like a drunken fuck-up, he reads like a flawed genius. The article was way more positive—and no doubt more interesting—than it would have been if Ryan drank nothing but chamomile tea that night in Chicago.

Ryan understood that if you were going to pass out on the sidewalk, it was cooler to do it with a music journalist standing over you. The kid was a freaking alley cat. No matter how bad he messed up or who he pissed off, he always landed on his feet.

"Our band is like a place you come to," Ryan told Gaurino at the beer garden, "and if you're strong enough, you stay there, and if you're not, you get the hell out." As the tour wound south, there were many times when I wondered if any of us—Ryan included—were strong enough to stay in Whiskeytown for long.

About a week after Chicago, we played a Nashville club called 12th & Porter. Like most of the shows since we'd started the RV tour, the crowd was in the 150 to 200 range—not huge, but considering that this was Whiskeytown's first headlining run, solid. And with "16 Days" getting strong radio play, plus a steady flow of press, it felt like the band was taking off. The Nashville show, though, like so many of the gigs on this tour, was a comedown.

After the band said goodnight, I stood at mix position talking to Bruce Neese, the long-haired, vampiric soundman. He looked sad. I asked him what was wrong.

"It's so depressing to stand here every night and watch this," he said in that gentle Georgia accent that was so at odds with his clothes and hair. He was a legit Whiskeytown fan, and it was killing him to watch them blow their opportunity. "This band could be so great. All they have to do is try. They've got these incredible songs, but they're pissing them away."

What could I say in return? Bruce was right.

After load-out, I herded everybody into the RV, and we drove to the hotel, a Super 8 far outside of downtown Nashville. It was about 2:00 a.m., long past closing time for the hotel pool, but we jumped the gate anyway. The band Hazeldine was touring with us at this point. A four-piece featuring three women and one guy, they'd been friends with Whiskeytown since the *No Depression* tour earlier that year. Sadly, in 2015 their bass player, Anne Tkach, would die in a St. Louis house fire. Ryan would write on Facebook that Anne "was always friendly, and always a great musician. I'll miss her on and off stage." Here in Tennessee, that tragedy was a long way off. The Hazeldine ladies were in the pool. Phil was in the pool. There was maybe some good-natured flirting between the two camps. Everybody was drinking and splashing and horsing around, enjoying the summer night.

There's an old joke that says La Quinta is Spanish for "The hotel next to the Denny's." Well, Super 8 is American English for "The hotel next to the Waffle House." And after an hour or so spent poolside, Ryan and I walked next door to get something to eat.

We tucked into a booth, the restaurant bustling like Waffle House always is: the waitresses taking orders and washing dishes and patronizing the drunks. The cooks working the grill and the waffle irons and the egg pans like conductors at the philharmonic. Waffle House is multitasking perfected. But compared to the mayhem of sound check, show, and load-out, it felt calm to me. Maybe because I wasn't on the clock.

After a while, Ryan looked across the table and said, "What do you think's gonna happen to me?"

I thought about it for a second. The kid was one of the smartest people I'd ever met. Probably a Mensa-level genius. Armed with more talent than you could ask for. But everything he built with one hand, he tore down with the other. Architect and wrecking ball all in one.

"I think you're like Tom Petty," I said. And I meant it. Ryan at twenty-two was that gifted a songwriter. "But I also think that Whiskeytown is like Petty's first band, Mudcrutch or whatever. It's gonna fizzle out eventually."

He looked down at his plate.

"But like Petty," I said, "you'll keep going. You're gonna do bigger and better things."

He looked up. "Are you gonna stick with me?"

I thought back to the record release show, to him playing "Avenues," to the two opposing routes his career might take, greatness or self-destruction. "I'll stick with you as long as you'll stick with me," I said.

"Okay," Ryan said. "Good."

No more second-guessing about taking this gig. I was in. Strapped to the rocket, whether it reached orbit or burst into flames before liftoff.

CHAPTER

A day or two later, we were loading into a radio station in Louisville. It was late afternoon, between sound check and showtime, and because the studio booth was small, we decided that Ryan and Caitlin should do the appearance alone. Whiskeytown in its fundamental form: Ryan on acoustic, Caitlin on fiddle.

We set up and went on the air. Cheesy DJ, in his overly professional radio voice, said to them, "So, you've got a new album out, huh?"

The musicians were sitting on stools, radio boom mics angling in front of them. "Yeah, man!" Ryan said. "We sure do! It's awesome!"

Diet Coke nearly shot out my nose. Ryan was aping Cheesy DJ's voice, mocking his put-on enthusiasm.

Cheesy DJ didn't seem to notice. He just smiled. "Are you going to play us a new song from that album?"

"Yeah!" Ryan said. "We're going to. But first, we've got a brand-new song we want to play. Something I just wrote on the drive over here."

Uh-oh. Ryan ad-libbing was trouble. I wondered if he was going to treat Louisville commuters to a song about his dirty laundry.

"Oh, wow," Cheesy DJ said, not realizing that Ryan was walking him right off the cliff. "A world exclusive. Right here."

Ryan looked at Caitlin, and they struck up a beautiful country ballad. Caitlin's fiddle weaving a brokenhearted melody over Ryan's strumming. They both looked serious as two chess players. Cheesy DJ closed his eyes and nodded along.

Ryan bent toward the mic. "Hey there, pretty little girl," he sang. "Don't you wanna smoke some crack with me?"

Cheesy DJ opened his eyes, fidgeted in his chair.

Ryan was singing his heart out, earnest as can be. "I promise you won't get addicted."

Apparently, they'd played "Don't You Wanna Smoke Some Crack with Me" on the *No Depression* tour, but this was the first time I'd heard it. And I loved it. And I loved Ryan Adams in that moment. This was a punk rock move, made even more so because it was sneaky rather than obvious. Any idiot could sing offensive lyrics on the radio, just come out middle-fingers-blazing. Ryan was smart enough to hide the middle finger inside a love song.

We didn't know it at the time, but as Ryan and Caitlin wound their way through a song about the joys of cocaine combustion, the station owner was driving around town, listening on his car radio. His kids were sitting in the backseat, probably just picked up from afterschool care. You can imagine one of them kicking the back of the driver's seat, asking, "Daddy, what's crack?"

As soon as the owner could get to a phone, he called the station and said, "Get them off the air!"

But by then, Ryan and Caitlin had already played a second song, and we'd headed off to the gig. Louisville was one of the very few radio in-studios Whiskeytown ever did. They all had a way of ending poorly.

The tour wound south toward Texas, a roller coaster of tight sets and loose sets, good drunks and bad hangovers. A fucked-up cirque du rock. One day's drive would be bad: two hundred miles of Ryan and Phil feuding. The next day's drive would be all laughter, the whole RV cracking up to a compilation tape of prank phone calls made by a North Carolina DJ named Charlie Whistlenut. The Lustre guys had introduced me to Whistlenut, and then I'd played the tape over and over for D Gen. Now, on the RV Tour, we listened to it all the time. Whistlenut, playing the part of a deep-woods redneck, making calls with titles like "Busted Front Winder" and "Keep Yer Pecker in Yer Pants." He ended every call by saying, "All right, we'll see ya." Ryan and the band thought the tape was so hilarious, we eventually ordered custom guitar pics with *WE'LL SEE YA* printed on them.

Still, the ups and downs were exhausting. For everyone. On the night Princess Diana died, we were in Memphis. Ryan's girlfriend Amy had flown in from New York to see him, and my girlfriend Stephanie had come in from Raleigh to see me. At some point, when all of us were out on Beale Street, barhopping and having a blast, Stephanie asked Caitlin how the tour was going.

"I just keep reminding myself," she said, "that in every city we play, they've got airplanes. If worse comes to worse, I can get a cab, head for the airport, and catch a ride home."

[71]

But worse wasn't coming to worse. In fact, once we got to Texas, worse was coming to better. As the *Fort Worth Star-Telegram* said, "Whiskeytown burned through an amazing set at the Dark Room in Dallas." Ryan was still drinking like a man going off to war, but he'd started to identify the edge of the envelope, pulling back on the stick before he crashed and burned. At the Dallas show, the *Star-Telegram* noticed: "Sucking on cigarettes, downing shots of liquor and taking requests from the very verbal audience, Adams delivered his poetic lyrics with a drunken but harmless swagger."

Drunken but harmless. Maybe Ryan had found his equilibrium.

Austin was even better than Dallas. If Chicago was alt-country's northern branch office, then surely Austin was the southern one. Over the last couple years, Ryan had become so enamored with Texas's capital city that after this leg of dates was over, he was going to move there. In fact, he'd already packed up his Raleigh apartment and shipped all his records and books to the Lone Star State.

In Austin, Whiskeytown shared the stage with Buick Mackane, the side project of legendary roots rock singer-songwriter Alejandro Escovedo. Alejandro had sung on several *Strangers Almanac* tracks, including a memorable lead vocal section on "Excuse Me While I Break My Own Heart Tonight," and since then he and Ryan had struck up a friendship.

Everybody who was anybody hung out that night, including Chris and Jenni from Jacknife. In the dressing room after the show, Ryan and Alejandro went mano a mano in a friendly songwriting duel. With a small crowd of insiders watching, Alejandro would play a tune on acoustic. Then Ryan would say, "Shoot, man. I have a better song than that." And he'd take a turn. Then it would go back to Alejandro. And back to Ryan. The kid was at his absolute best in settings like this, where the emphasis was on craft instead of performance. He was witty, charming, self-deprecating—and he took songwriting dead seriously. That night's proper show had been really good, but the virtuoso set happened backstage after the bands said goodnight. If Alejandro's wife hadn't eventually broken it up, he and Ryan might have been trading songs come sunrise.

We left Texas and motored west across New Mexico and Arizona to Los Angeles, where we were booked for two nights at The Mint. I'd decided we needed a temporary break from staying in Super 8s on the wrong side of the outerbelt. In Los Angeles, we treated ourselves to three days at Le Rêve, a boutique hotel (now called the Petit Ermitage) in West Hollywood, between Sunset and Santa Monica, just down the hill from the Viper Room. One day, when I walked down to the lobby, Stevie Wonder was standing there with his entourage, waiting for the elevator. His people let me ride up first. Alone.

Those three days surrounding the shows were filled with instances like that, L.A. moments, real rock star stuff. Hanging out on Sunset Strip, staring up at the Hollywood hills from the rooftop pool, schmoozing with the Outpost Records brass. Everybody was on their best behavior. Nobody puked up salsa or passed out on the sidewalk. Los Angeles was a reminder of how fan-freaking-tastic being on a major label could be. And maybe, starting now, *would* be.

Same thing in San Francisco, where the show at Bottom of the Hill was stellar. And in Eugene, where for an encore Ryan came out by himself, sat down behind Steven's drums, and started singing the melody of "Sweet Home Alabama," except all the words were about baking biscuits at Hardee's. And in Seattle, alt-country's western branch office and home of *No Depression* magazine. A month earlier, when the tour was first getting off the ground, Whiskeytown *were* rookies, just as that heckler in Boston had recognized. But now, man, they'd settled into a groove. And it was great.

Still, every day on that tour started with the Herculean task of me attempting to get everybody out of the hotel and into the RV. After staying up drinking until 2:00 or 3:00 in the morning, it was nearly impossible to get the camper loaded by 11:00 or noon or whatever time was necessary for us to drive the miles that lay between us and sound check. Caitlin was always on time for the morning RV call, and Mike Daly wasn't far behind her, but the others were seasoned lollygaggers. Come the designated hour, Caitlin would be standing outside, reading a book. But there'd be no Ryan. Or maybe Ryan would be there, but there'd be no Phil or Steven. Then I'd have to go upstairs and bang on a hotel room door. I'd finally get Phil and Steven downstairs, but by then Chris Laney would have gotten sick of waiting and disappeared himself.

One Saturday, Bruce Neese and I were standing in the hotel parking lot, prepping the RV for the drive. Ryan was up in the loft of the camper, having already fallen back asleep. Caitlin was leaning against the RV, drinking coffee with Chris Laney and Mike Daly. But no Phil, no Steven. I went to the front desk to ask for a key to their room. When I opened the door, I found each of them stretched out on a bed, shirtless, with towels wrapped around their waists. They looked like they'd just gotten out of a sauna.

"What the hell are you doing?" I said. "We gotta get out of here."

Both of them kept their eyes on the TV, where a college football game was about to kick off.

"No way, man," Steven said, nestling deeper into the bed. "West Virginia's playing." He actually thought we were going to wait to leave until the Mountaineers notched a victory.

Eventually we'd roll out, maybe an hour late. And then, of course, thirty minutes into the drive, somebody from the back would say, "Man, I'm hungry." So we'd stop, get something to eat, and that would take an hour. We'd drive another sixty miles, and my SkyPager would go off. Maybe it was important, like Chris Roldan calling to say Ryan was supposed to do a phone interview. Or maybe it was just Stephanie calling to tell me the cat threw up. Either way, I'd have to pull into a truckstop and answer the page. There was no such thing as running inside to do a quick phone call. Everybody had to follow me. After I got off the phone, it would take half an hour to get them back into the RV and away from the racks of Elvis sunglasses and trucker caps and t-shirts that read *My Two Favorite Daniels: Jack and Charlie.*

Needless to say, we were late for sound check every night. So every morning I tried to set the RV call a little earlier, but the earlier I aimed for, the later they were. It was like a Chinese finger trap: the harder I pulled them out of the hotel, the more they stayed stuck inside.

One day during that West Coast swing, I had to wake up Ryan and Phil so they could do a phone interview with an East Coast magazine.

"Why'd we schedule this thing so early?" Phil said, sitting up from the bed and planting his feet on the floor.

"Dude," I said. "It's 2:00 in the afternoon."

Phil was not impressed. "If that magazine wants to talk to us," he said, "they can wait until *we* are ready to talk to *them.*"

"Oh, really," I said.

He was now upright and walking. "They need us more than we need them."

"I understand that, Phil," I said, now in full placate-the-rock-star mode, "But here's the problem." I reminded him that the United States has four time zones. 2:00 p.m. here on the West Coast meant 5:00 p.m. back east. "That writer in New York wants to go home and see his family. He doesn't want to wait until 8:00 at night to talk to you. You've got to make it easy for him." I tossed a shirt his way. "And believe me," I said. "You need him more than he needs you. There's a hundred other bands this guy could be talking to, bands that have sold a lot more records than you."

"Outpost doesn't care about record sales," he said. "They signed us because they needed a cool band on their roster."

We were late for interview. There was no time to explain that his record label was—exactly as advertised—in the business of selling records, that it was a subsidiary of Universal Music Group, which itself was a subsidiary of Seagram's (yep, the beverage company). Multinational corporations answered to *Wall Street Journal*-reading shareholders, not hungover guitar players. Corporations only care about *cool* to the extent that it adds to the bottom line. Weeks later, I told Outpost's Mark Williams that Phil said the record company didn't care about record sales. He busted out laughing.

This was my bottom line: my job was to deliver the band to sound check on time, and I was failing. So even though the shows were getting progressively better, I was worried that I was getting progressively closer to fired. I tried to explain my dilemma to the band this way: the reason you leave for the airport early is so that if there's a traffic jam, you don't miss your flight. You account for the mishap that hopefully won't happen. Just to be safe. Likewise, we needed to leave for the gigs early just in case something went wrong.

If we were lucky, everything would be fine, and we'd show up for load-in early.

"You know, guys," I said, "there's no shame in being early." But over the next couple weeks, nothing changed. We were late as ever.

Finally, on the drive from Seattle to Portland, something did go wrong. We were headed south on I-5, past Tacoma and Olympia, when *bam!-flap-flap-flap*. Flat tire. I limped the RV over to the shoulder and climbed down to inspect the damage, traffic dopplering past at freeway speed. One of the four back wheels had punctured. Even with a 75 percent operable back axle—and with the RV now listing to port—I could still drive it. Barely.

A few miles down the interstate, we found a truckstop with a repair shop. The mechanic fixed the flat, but it was now long past load-in, and we were still fifty miles from the club. When we finally pulled up to the place—Berbati's Pan, it was called—the doors were open, and the opening band was about to go on. This was the latest we'd ever been. We loaded right through the audience and straight onto the stage. Portland ended up being a great show (I remember Phil smoking pot right in the open during the between-song lulls), but I'd had enough of the cat herding. I was fucking furious.

The next day, on the way to Boise, where we had a day off, we drove I-84 along the Columbia River. We stopped at Multnomah Falls. Craned our necks up at Mount Hood. Shook our heads at the daredevils kiteboarding the Columbia Gorge. The scenery was beautiful, but I was still steaming about how late we'd been the night before. At a gas station later that afternoon, I gathered everybody around. "Look," I said. "Here's the deal. I'm *this close* to getting fired."

"No, dude," Phil said. "We're the band. The only people who can fire you is *us*."

Ryan nodded. "The label and managers have got nothing to do with it."

"I know you think that," I said, "but you're wrong. It's my job to make sure you don't show up for sound check six hours late."

"But we love you," Caitlin said. "We need you."

"Thank you," I said. "I appreciate you saying that. But if I can't get you to the shows on time, the record company is going to find somebody who can. That's how this business works."

I told them that starting now, things were going to run differently. When we got to Boise, I was going to get an extra key for every room. The extra keys were mine. No more pounding on doors. And tomorrow morning, I said, everybody was going to report to the RV at 9:00 a.m. sharp. Anybody who wasn't there? I'd open the door to their room and dump an ice bucket of water on their face. "And there's not one person in this RV who can beat my ass," I said. "I'm bigger than all of you."

It took the threat of physical violence, but once I got that tirade out of my system, I felt a whole lot better. In Boise, we drank at a karaoke bar, and I had a stack of hotel key cards in my wallet. Unfortunately Ryan didn't have his ID in his wallet, and when the Boise bouncer carded him, Ryan couldn't prove he was of legal drinking age. He stormed back to the RV. The rest of us, however, had a great time. When Caitlin's name came up on the karaoke sheet, she took the mic and sang Tammy Wynette's "D-I-V-O-R-C-E."

Looking back now on that song selection, it was like she knew what would soon happen.

After Boise, we played Denver and Boulder, then we spent an off day in Lawrence, Kansas. The next day, everything started out fine. When we checked out of the hotel, everybody was in a good mood, and everybody made it out to the parking lot on time for the short afternoon drive to Kansas City. We got to the club early, a place called the Hurricane. Phil, Chris, and Steven grabbed a pre-sound-check beer at the bar. When I couldn't find Ryan come sound-check time, I discovered that he wasn't passed out on the sidewalk in front of the club; he was sitting in the alley behind the venue, next to a dumpster, with his acoustic across his lap.

"Man," he said, standing up and dusting himself off, "I just wrote a great new song." Walking with me into the club, he was still stoked about the new tune.

I looked at the six Whiskeytowners on stage: everybody on time, in tune, and doing what they were supposed to be doing. Everything was pretty fine. Maybe Ryan and Phil were arguing a little bit, but that was business-as-usual for them. There was no reason to expect anything out of the ordinary.

The show was solid. The band powered through the set, and everything was going well. After an hour or so, they kicked into "Today," a new song they'd been closing with recently. Figuring that this was the end of the set, I started packing up the guitars, mentally congratulating myself for getting another Whiskeytown show in the books. I was one step further from fired.

But then I noticed that Ryan wasn't singing the usual lyrics to "Today." He was making up stuff on the fly. This wasn't necessarily cause for alarm. Maybe he was singing about laundry; maybe he was singing about Hardee's biscuits. By now I'd come to love the Ryan Adams impromptu. I was standing off to the side, at stage right, so I was only getting the words through the monitors, not through the front-of-house speakers. I couldn't understand what he was saying, but I knew it wasn't the regular words. I stopped putting away the gear and slid closer to the monitors. Suddenly I could hear. I got it.

He was turning "Today" into a diatribe against the music business, listing everything he hated about the road, everything that sucked about being in a band. Shit. This wasn't a playful freestyle about doing laundry or baking biscuits. This was serious.

Now I was worried. But the song kept going. The band was jamming, adding solos, while Ryan sang verse after verse, complaining about how shitty his life in the music biz was. None of this had been planned; they were obviously winging it, everybody trying to keep up with Ryan. After a while, Ryan stopped singing, and Phil went off on an extended, improvised guitar solo. The solo kept going. And going. Finally, Ryan brought the song to a close with an arena-style ending, everyone grinding down on one big chord, Steven filling the stage with a wash of cymbals. I stood at stage right with my mouth open, thinking, *What the fuck is happening?*

With a mighty crash, "Today" ended. Ryan took off his guitar and let it clang to the ground. Then he walked up to the mic and said to the audience, "Go home and get on the fucking Internet and tell your friends you just saw the last Whiskeytown show."

What? Where did this come from? Surely he didn't mean it. This tour had been a series of ups and downs, and Ryan and Phil had been tweaking each other and fighting in that brotherly way, but there'd been no hint that he was going to explode the whole operation. We'd just gotten started.

Ryan angled offstage, heading straight for me with a look on his face that was heart-attack-serious. I was used to him being some combination of drunken, silly, and sad. *Stern* was a first. "I don't care what you have to do to make it happen," he said, "but I have to be back in Jacksonville, North Carolina, tomorrow." Then he walked out the door.

The crowd filed out of the Hurricane in stunned silence. Everyone in the band was confused. *What did he say? Does this mean we're broken up for real?*

Chris Laney and Mike Daly caught up to Ryan outside. "Come on, dude," Chris said. "This band is great. We can't quit now."

"Yeah, man," Mike Daly pleaded. "Come on."

But Ryan walked away.

While Caitlin left to go call Skillet, Phil and everybody else went to the bar. "Fuck him," Phil said.

Not knowing what else to do, I got to work packing up the gear. Last show or not, somebody had to get the shit off the stage and into the RV.

A while later, Ryan walked up to me. "Come here," he said. "I need you."

I followed him out of the club and across the street to a rundown gas station. On the periphery of the lot stood a pay phone. The handset was hanging straight down. Somebody had obviously been "on hold" for a long time. Ryan picked up the phone and gave it to me. By now he was clearly drunk. "Talk to her," he said. And then he disappeared.

It was his ex-girlfriend Melanie, from back in Raleigh. She wanted to know what was going on. She said she was worried about him. He didn't sound right. I told her what had happened at the show, but I didn't know anything else. I wasn't even sure why he'd put me on the phone with her. I'd heard him talk about Melanie, but I had never met her. This is the first time we'd ever spoken. After an awkward few minutes, I hung up and went back inside to deal with the club.

On the half-hour drive to the Super 8, everybody was hammered, everybody was mad. We'd go five or ten miles in near silence, all of us simmering in our own private anger. Then, like a pot boiling over, somebody would work themselves up to a rage, let out a loud *fuck you*, which would lead to a barrage of counter-*fuck you*s, and then it would settle back to steaming silence until the pot boiled over again. On that long drive, one thing was obvious: Ryan wasn't kidding around. He meant what he'd said. Whiskeytown as we knew it was over.

Strangers Almanac had been out for only two months.

At the hotel, Ryan fumed up to his room. In the parking lot, Phil, Chris, and Steven were throwing a football and drinking beer. I walked up to them and asked how they were doing.

Phil gave me a big hug. "I love you, man," he said, squeezing tight. He was the only person in the band who was my height. "Thanks for all your hard work."

Then on the hotel pay phone I dialed up the Jacknife office number. Back in May, my career with Ryan Adams had begun with a call from Chris Roldan. Now, four months later, with a call to that same number, my Whiskeytown days were apparently ending.

It was 3:00 a.m. Their machine answered. "Nobody's dead," I said to the voice mailbox, "but as soon as you wake up, you need to call me."

PART

2

I Played in Whiskeytown and All I Got Was This Lousy Goddamn T-shirt! (Fall 1997–Spring 1998)

CHAPTER

Caitlin and I stayed up until daybreak talking to Ryan, trying to get him to finish the tour. There were four shows still to play on this leg. After that, reevaluate. But Ryan wouldn't budge. He insisted that Whiskeytown was done.

I went back to my room, sat on the bed, and looked at my calendar. In a couple of weeks the band was supposed set out on a two-month jaunt through the eastern United States. As the sun rose over Kansas City, I was looking at a long list of gigs. And no band to play them.

A few hours later, I woke to the buzzing of my pager. It was Jacknife calling from Austin. "Okay," I said to Chris and Jenni when I got them on the phone, "here's the thing . . ."

Soon I had them speaking directly with Ryan, and after hours of frustrating back and forth (long enough for me to take a full nap), Jenni and Chris convinced Ryan not to retreat to Jacksonville after all. Rather than cancel the rest of that leg, he and Caitlin would finish the dates as a duo. I'd travel with the two-piece. The rest of the band would go back to North Carolina. Their tour was over. Given his history of arguing with Ryan, I wasn't entirely surprised that Phil had been shit-canned, but I sure didn't expect it to happen onstage. Plus his name was on the record contract. Firing him was going to involve lawyers. As for Steven, Chris, and Mike Daly getting the boot, I was very surprised. They seemed like innocent bystanders.

While everybody else tried to sleep, I took a taxi out to the airport, where I rented a minivan. I was still shell-shocked, concentrating on the logistics of getting Ryan and Caitlin to the next show so that I didn't have to think too hard about the bomb that had just gone off. Back at the hotel, I loaded the new ride with two acoustic guitars, Caitlin's fiddle, and our suitcases. Then I handed Bruce Neese a wad of cash and the keys to the RV. "Get these guys home," I said.

Caitlin, Ryan, and I headed east in the vehicle of choice for soccer moms everywhere. Meanwhile, Bruce drove Phil, Steven, Chris, and Mike Daly to Raleigh. They covered the thousand miles in one straight shot and then dropped the RV off at my house, leaving the keys and paperwork with Stephanie. After nearly two months in Whiskeytown's possession, the Jamboree Searcher by Fleetwood Mac was trashed. The seat cushions were pocked with cigarette burn holes. There were scuff and scrape marks everywhere. A week later, when I returned the RV to the Cruise America office, the manager shook his head, gave me a tsk-tsk-tsk, and billed me an extra fifteen hundred in damages.

But first I needed to get Ryan and Caitlin through the last four gigs. That night, we were supposed to appear in St. Louis, but as we drove toward the Gateway City, neither of them was in the right frame of mind to play a show. We all felt raw and wrung-out. The wreckage from the breakup was still smoldering. So I cancelled

St. Louis. That night we sped right past the Arch and over the Mississippi without stopping. That left three shows: Louisville, Nashville, and Huntsville.

When we showed up in Louisville the next day, the promoter eyeballed the minivan. "Where's the band?" he said. He kept looking though the side doors, as if he stared hard enough, more musicians would clown-car out of them.

I nodded toward Ryan and Caitlin. "This *is* the band."

"What the fuck?" he said. He was mad. It was Friday night. He'd been promised a six-piece rock band, not a folk duo. By his math, 66.6 percent of Whiskeytown was missing. But the promoter didn't know what I knew: that Ryan and Caitlin were the only percentage of Whiskeytown that truly mattered.

"Here's what we're going to do," I said to the guy. I told him to put a sign on the door that read *Whiskeytown will be performing tonight as a duo.* "If anyone wants their money back, give it to them. Then deduct it from our pay at the end of the night."

The show was great. In Louisville, the city where bourbon flows as strong as the Ohio River, Whiskeytown was distilled down to purity. Ryan and Caitlin were funny and self-deprecating. The set was much longer, more interesting, and more sober than it would have been if the full band had still been around. And not one person asked for their money back. As the doors flew open, even the promoter smiled. *Long live Whiskeytown*, I thought as I loaded the guitars and fiddle into the minivan. *Be it dead or alive.*

In between shows, as we made our way from Louisville to Nashville to Huntsville, we weren't just covering miles; we were reconstituting the band, building the lineup that would play the long tour that started in two short weeks.

"So who's gonna play drums?" I said from behind the wheel. Ryan didn't hesitate. "I want Skillet."

Skillet Gilmore was the band's original drummer, the guy who'd quit just before Ryan and Phil signed with Outpost. He was also Caitlin's boyfriend. "All right, Caitlin," I said. "At the next gas station, we're going to stop so you can call Skillet."

We stopped. Caitlin called. "Okay," she said, climbing back into the van. "Skillet's in." I didn't know it yet, but Skillet would later say that the reason he came back is because Phil was gone.

"Good," I said. Now Whiskeytown was a three-piece. "Who's gonna be the lapsteel/keyboard player? We need a utility man."

Ryan hedged. "I don't know. Somebody great."

I reminded him that Mike Daly was great. And he was the only lapsteel player we knew that a.) wasn't seventy years old and b.) didn't live in a shack in the holler. I campaigned on Mike Daly's behalf for twenty miles.

"You're right," Ryan finally said. "Let's go with Mike Daly."

We stopped, left a message on Mike Daly's answering machine in New Jersey, and a few hours later, he said yes. Whiskeytown was a four-piece.

Now we were down to the guitar and bass positions. Ryan was adamant that Phil wasn't coming back. As he'd later tell the *Phoenix New Times*, Phil "wasn't happy being in the band, but he wouldn't quit. The only way for him to leave was if somebody made him, so I made him."

Ryan and his attorney would eventually settle with Phil, officially removing him from the record contract and axing him from the band.

Here in the minivan, Ryan decided that he wanted Ed Crawford to take the lead guitar spot. Also known as ed fROMOHIO,

Crawford been one-third (along with Mike Watt and George Hurley) of the seminal punk band fIREHOSE. Ed was, in fact, from Ohio, and although fIREHOSE had been based in San Pedro, California, he had been living in Chapel Hill of late, fronting Grand National, a band that featured Jon Wurster from Superchunk on drums.

I knew that Ed was an amazing guitar player, one who would bring a walletful of indie-rock credibility with him. I also knew that he was much older than Ryan, about the same age as me. I wondered if a punk rock veteran like Ed would have the patience to tour with a bunch of greenhorns. "Will he do it?" I asked Ryan.

Ryan shrugged. "I'll call him."

Another gas station. Another phone call. Ed told Ryan yes, he would do it—but he wanted his girlfriend, Jenni Snyder, who played with Ed and Jon Wurster in Grand National, to join Whiskeytown as the bass player.

"Is she any good?" I asked.

"She's awesome," Ryan said. "And it'd be great to have another girl in the band."

Sounded like a deal to me. Buy one guitar player, get one bass player free. By the time we got to Huntsville to do the last of the three acoustic shows, Whiskeytown Mark II was set.

So far, the band was batting two-for-two as a Ryan/Caitlin duo. In Nashville we'd done the same thing as Louisville: the promoter put a sign on the door, everybody was happy, and nobody wanted a refund. *No Depression*'s Grant Alden would later rave about the show, writing, "What was truly a surprise, and may yet prove a blessing, was how beautifully Cary and Adams carried off a set of songs that went on and on and on until the bar stopped serving. It was a far cry from the pleasant but somehow perfunctory rock shows the band had offered up a few weeks earlier in Atlanta." Alden noted that Ryan was "exposed, nervous, and energized," and that he turned in "a powerfully vulnerable performance."

I agreed. Louisville and Nashville were the best I'd seen Ryan since backstage in Austin, when he'd done that friendly duel with Alejandro Escovedo, and before that, when he'd played "Avenues" solo at the album release show. As far as I was concerned, Ryan and Caitlin could just keep playing as a duo.

In Huntsville, however, Ryan announced to Caitlin and me that he wasn't going to play the show, period. He didn't say why; he just said no. This was a big, outdoor festival, with the Nixons and a few more guitar-heavy acts on the bill. My guess was that because we'd now cobbled together a new lineup, the thought of playing as an acoustic duo in the open air for two-thousand drunk Alabamans wasn't so exciting for Ryan. He'd already grown bored of the two-piece and was ready to move on to the next edition of the full band.

"Look, man," I said. "You gotta do it. Let's just finish the tour like we said we would."

He shook his head. "I don't want to."

Suddenly a motivational tactic came to me. Ryan hated airplanes back then. Flying scared him shitless. I could remember several times when he'd checked his bag at the counter, walked down the Jetway, and then, right before the flight attendants closed the door, he'd panicked and gotten off the plane. His unaccompanied suitcase would arrive in Raleigh at the scheduled time, and I'd have to make a trip to the airport to claim it. But Ryan wouldn't arrive until a day later. At the bus station.

I offered him a deal. If he played the Huntsville show, I'd drive him in the minivan to Austin, the town he was in the process of moving to, where all his belongings were waiting. "But if you cancel," I said, "You're taking the Greyhound to Austin. Two long, hot days on a cramped bus."

"All right," he said. "I'll do it." And even though the show was big and outdoors—not the kind of intimate environment where a nuanced acoustic set typically shines—Ryan and Caitlin were fantastic. The frontman and guitar player of the Nixons watched the set from the side of the stage, both of them singing along with Ryan the whole time. *Strangers Almanac* had now been in stores for two months, and it seemed like most music people—bands, DJs, industry reps—had heard the record and were digging it.

The next day, I drove Caitlin to the airport. She'd spent much of the tour assuring herself that she could always fly home if things got too bad, and now I was dropping her off curbside at the end of that tour. We said good-bye, and then, as promised, Ryan and I minivanned to Austin.

From there I flew back to Raleigh. We'd been gone for two months. I'd done longer tours before, but never one that was so emotionally exhausting. I was thrilled to be back in the Triangle and back with Stephanie.

But I wasn't home for long. I landed in Raleigh on the first of October. The next tour would begin in Richmond in two weeks. In the meantime, the new lineup (Ryan, Caitlin, Skillet, Mike Daly, Ed, and Jenni) flew to Austin, where they met up with Ryan for a week of rehearsals. While they worked on the music, I worked on the tour preparations.

First I had a long talk with Chris and Jenni from Jacknife, I told them we needed a tour bus. Not a van, not an RV. A full-on bus, like the kind Kevin Cronin from REO had. The RV experience had left us with rock-and-roll PTSD. It would be a long time before anybody in Whiskeytown would be ready to step into in another RV. For years afterward, any time I was forced to enter an RV (like at an outdoor festival, say, where they were using an RV as a production office), I'd have a Whiskeytown flashback and feel sick, like I might just puke up a burrito. If the band had any hope of staying together until the end of this tour, I told Chris and Jenni, we needed space. Space meant a bus.

Compared to Ryan and Whiskeytown, I was the touring professional, but the truth was, I only had a little more experience than they did. For all the roadwork I'd done to that point, I had never managed a bus tour. My knowledge of buses was limited to the school bus I drove when I was in the tenth grade.

Let me say that again: I *drove* the bus that brought me and my buddies to school.

In North Carolina when I was a kid, districts would allow sixteen-year-olds to be school bus operators. Sounded sweet to me. I already worked at McDonalds, but I wanted to make more money. So a few weeks after I turned sixteen, I signed up for the bus-driving gig. I took a weeklong class, passed the road and written tests, and *bam*, I had my bus driver's license. I was suddenly in charge of delivering all the kids in my neighborhood to school.

I would wake up early, and the bus would be parked in my driveway, right where I'd left it the afternoon before. I'd fire it up, back out of the drive, and head out on my route, covering the east side of Lake Norman, picking up the young scholars of South Iredell High. For the next ninety minutes, I would circle the lake, swinging down and around curvy roads, slipping in and out of cove after cove. Then I'd drop off my classmates, park the bus at a lot on the school grounds, grab my backpack, and head inside.

I know this sounds crazy today. Believe me, I thought it was crazy even then.

There was a group of four or five potheads that rode the bus. Every morning, I would drop them off near a grove of trees that was at the start of a long dirt road. After they disappeared into the woods, I'd drive down the dirt road and pick up the kids who lived back in there. That would take maybe ten minutes. Then I'd do a U-turn and circle back. The potheads would come out of the woods and get back on the bus. Maybe they smelled like weed. I couldn't tell. The bus would already be too choked with cigarette smoke.

Once, on exam day, I intentionally drove the bus into a ditch and got it stuck—just so we all would have an excuse to be late for our tests. Another day, I looked into the rearview and saw there was a fight breaking out in back. I turned toward the fifteen-year-old kid who always sat up front, and I said, "You ready?" He lived at the end of my route, and a few times when he was the last one left on the bus, I'd let him take a turn driving. So now, without stopping, I slid out from behind the wheel and he took my place. "Be right back," I said to him. And I walked down the aisle to go break up the fight.

When they saw me standing there, the tension instantly diffused "What the fuck are you doing back here?" one of the would-be-brawlers said.

"Breaking up you dipshits," I said.

He looked up to the front of the bus. The color drained from his face. "If you're here, then who's driving?"

Now that I think about it, driving that bus was the start of my career as a tour manager. Appease the potheads, break up the fights, get everybody where they're supposed to be. That's what I've been doing ever since.

Waiting to Derail

After getting the okay from Jacknife to go ahead with the bus rental, I still had a million questions about how it all worked, so I called my tour-manager buddies for advice. I found out that on a bus, there are different rules, different considerations, a different vocabulary. *Make sure the driver gets enough sleep. Make sure the venue sets out cones to reserve a place to park. Sleep with your feet pointed toward the front, so if the driver slams the breaks, you don't snap your neck. You can piss, but you can't shit. You don't stop for gas; you stop for fuel. If you get off the bus at a truck stop at night, you'd better let the driver know, or else while you're still in the bathroom zipping your pants, the bus'll be merging back on to the Interstate.*

Thanks to the bus, we would have space for an extra crew guy. I called up my buddy Ace, a kid I'd known since our days at South Iredell High, when he'd sit on the bench behind the driver's seat, smoking cigarettes on the ride to school. He had sold merch for me with Lustre, and he'd guitar-teched for D Generation. His real name was Dana, but he hated that name, so he went by Ace. He claimed that his nickname was a reference to his skill with the ladies, but I suspect he actually meant Ace as in Frehley, from KISS. He was a good friend, and I knew he'd work just for the per diem, no salary. Best of all, having Ace around would mean less time humping gear for me, more time dealing with promoters, managers, and label reps. In addition to Ace, I'd also recruited a new soundman, John Clark, who we all called JC. He was a Chapel Hill guy who'd done a long run with the Squirrel Nut Zippers. As the first date approached, I knew that crew-wise we were in good shape. I hoped the same could be said for the musicians, who were down in Texas, supposedly working up the set.

The plan was for me to fly to Austin, meet up with the bus and driver, and then grab Ryan and the band. The bus would take all of us to Charlotte to get Ace, stop in Chapel Hill to pick up JC, and then we'd be off to Richmond for the first show.

I landed in Austin and took a taxi to a downtown hotel. Parked right out front was a gleaming Silver Eagle. I considered myself a van guy at heart, but I have to admit, walking up to the bus, knowing that it was waiting for me, I was pumped. In its forty-five-foot-long promise of debauchery and depravity, a tour bus was rock-stardom in vehicle form.

Standing on the sidewalk next to the Silver Eagle were a man and a woman who looked to be in their midfifties. The guy had long hair and a serious beard—maybe not ZZ Top serious but close. He wore a Southwestern jacket with lots of beads and fringe, and his jewelry added up to probably a pound of turquoise. This dude was our driver. He introduced himself as Uncle Donnie. The woman next to him was his wife.

"I've been tour-managing for years," I told Uncle Donnie, "but I've never rented a bus. If I do something wrong, let me know."

"Son," he said, "Let me tell you what . . ." And in a voice that reminded me of Foghorn Leghorn, he spent the next fifteen minutes breaking down in intricate detail the ways in which he'd swindled the tour manager of the last band he'd worked with. Back then drivers were paid strictly in cash, and Uncle Donnie made it clear that he knew all the angles. I didn't know why he was telling me, but I knew one thing: despite my homework, I was way out of my league.

That afternoon we met up with Ryan and the band. Shaking Jenni Snyder's hand, I realized that although I'd never been officially introduced to our new bass player, I had seen her before. One of those times when I'd gone to Ryan's apartment to wake him up for something, there had been a girl passed out, fully clothed, in his bed.

That girl was Jenni. How her relationship with Ryan fit into her supposed relationship with Ed, I had no idea. It was too late to worry about romantic entanglements. We had shows to do. We loaded the guitars, drums, amps, and keyboards into the luggage bays of the bus. The gear barely fit, but we Tetrised it in. No trailer necessary. Self-contained in the Silver Eagle. With a hiss of the hydraulics, Whiskeytown rolled out of Austin, heading for the East Coast.

Ed Crawford and I had stocked the bus with a bunch of beer and snacks, and out here on I-35, cruising along at 70 mph, the launch party was kicking off. Everybody was in a great mood. Cracking beers. Wide-eyed about traveling by bus and superexcited about how the band was sounding. It felt like a new beginning. A better beginning. And to think: two weeks earlier, all that remained of Whiskeytown could fit in a minivan.

Ed and I sat in the back lounge, smoking cigarettes and tying on a buzz. There we were, two guys in our thirties. Born just four days apart. Ed had toured all over the United States and Europe with fIREHOSE. I'd toured all over the United States and Europe with ANTiSEEN. But for both of us, this was our first bus. I looked down the aisle at Ryan, who was smiling and joking and acting like the kid he was. Still just twenty-two, and yet his instincts were already honed. Just as he understood that if you're going to pass out drunk on the sidewalk, make sure a reporter is watching, he also knew that you got more attention for firing the band on stage in Kansas City than you did waiting until everybody got safely home. He also realized that that kind of attention wouldn't hobble his career; it would propel it.

I couldn't help but admire Ryan. The kid was a rock-and-roll savant, with way more natural talent than me, Ed, or anybody else

I knew. Still, part of me was disappointed that he didn't appreciate how good he had it. How lucky he was. How quickly all this success had come. In an eye-blink he'd gone from writing songs on a bar napkin to chugging Budweiser on a tour bus.

I took a long swig of beer. Stretched my legs on the back lounge sofa. I looked down the aisle at the kids, who were smiling and having a ball. Turning toward Ed, I laughed. "You know what?" I said. "We're the only ones that really earned this."

CHAPTER

After gigs in Richmond and Baltimore, Uncle Donnie motored the Silver Eagle into Manhattan for a coheadlining show at Irving Plaza with the Old 97's. The Dallas-based 97's had released their major-label debut, *Too Far to Care*, in June, a month before *Strangers Almanac* came out. Now it was October, and they were sitting neck-and-neck with Whiskeytown on the alt-country totem pole. The two bands had appeared together at SXSW 1996, and ever since, Ryan had been trying to start a public feud with the band and their frontman, Rhett Miller. Miller was like Ryan in reverse: Ryan was punk; Miller was pop. Ryan was drunk; Miller was not. Ryan would often say, "Rhett wears white pants, and I wear black pants. That's the difference between the two bands." In Ryan's mind, the year was 1967 and Whiskeytown was the Rolling Stones. The Old 97's were the Dave Clark Five. He knew that an interband rivalry would play in the press, so over the last year and a half—while opening for the Old 97's on the *No Depression* tour and in various magazine interviews—

he had talked an inordinate amount of shit about Miller, which the Dallas singer-songwriter mostly laughed off.

The day before the Irving Plaza show, Ryan set up shop in Geffen's New York offices and did a round of press interviews. He wasted no time digging into the Old 97's, telling a reporter from Pittsburgh: "They're going to get shown up. We're excited about seeing them walk onstage and take on fake Texas accents. It's a sort of Oasis/Blur-type rivalry, but we're better. And I'll keep this up if it means it'll sell more records for them."

Ryan hated sports, but he sure could rise to the level of the competition. The next night at the show, Whiskeytown was on fire. It was only the third gig with the new lineup: Ed Crawford on guitar, Jenni Snyder on bass, and Skillet Gilmore back on drums to complement Ryan, Caitlin, and Mike Daly. The set was short, but with the addition of Ed's ballsy playing, it packed a wallop.

We headed into the Midwest to do shows in Pennsylvania and Ohio, and the new cast of characters made for a new band dynamic. Caitlin and Skillet were dating, so they mostly hung out as a couple. Then you had Ed and Jenni, who'd definitely dated back in Chapel Hill, but even though they were spending a lot of time drinking together, I couldn't tell if they were still romantically linked. Some days they acted like a couple, some days not. To me it seemed like Jenni was interested in Ryan. And vice versa. There was definitely flirting going on between Jenni and Ryan. She was in her midtwenties, so Ryan was close to her age, whereas Ed was an older dude like me. Plus I'd seen her at Ryan's apartment in a few months earlier. Now on the bus, I wondered if maybe their flirting wasn't *just* flirting.

Whenever the two couples—Caitlin and Skillet, Ed and Jenni—were paired off, Ryan and Mike Daly hung out together. Mike Daly was ambitious, and by now, three months into his stint with the band, he realized that hitching himself to the Adams train might be a very good (and profitable) idea. So he tried to make himself invaluable to Ryan. The new lineup sounded great, but it felt volatile. Anything that got built that quickly might get broken just as quickly. If Ryan one day decided to do a Kansas City repeat and dynamite the whole thing, Mike Daly wanted to make sure he was standing outside the blast radius, alongside the guy with the plunger and the TNT. I can't blame Mike Daly for betting his chips on Ryan. I was doing the same thing. We all were.

Why wouldn't we want to stay on this carnival ride for as long as we could? Sure Ryan could be infuriating, but for every drunken shitshow like the Double Door, there was a brilliant moment like when he played the "Avenues" solo. Beyond his talent, there was the magnetic force of his personality. When he was in a good mood, he was funny and charismatic, great to hang around with. You'd spend most of the time doubled over with laughter. Talk with Ryan for five minutes, and you immediately learned how quick and articulate he was. He was probably one of the funniest people I'd ever met. He was definitely one of the smartest people I'd ever met. I have no doubt that if he got a good night's sleep, drank a cup of coffee, and then tried hard on a proper IQ test, he'd score at the genius level. Not "genius" in a euphemistic sense, like, "Oh, man, that guy's a genius," but a certified, 98th-percentile genius.

Whenever the topic of conversation was something he was passionate about—a record he'd heard, a book he'd read, a movie he'd seen—he was so knowledgeable and thoughtful. On the other hand, when the topic was something he didn't care about—like basic history or geography—then he was equally impressive in the opposite direction. His ignorance was just as mind-blowing as his intelligence. Oftentimes, if you're world-class good at one thing, then you're world-class bad at something else. Just as Einstein could determine the theory of relativity but forget to comb his hair, Ryan could write a sophisticated, mournful song like "Dancing With the Women at the Bar" and still think that Chicago sits on the Gulf of Mexico.

When you rubbed the height of Ryan's intelligence up against the depth of his ignorance, you got friction, tension, conflict. Those three combined to make *drama*, and drama was the fuel that powered him. As tour manager, drama was the last thing I wanted. I liked routine and predictable. I liked normal. Ryan hated normal. Normal made him itchy. So if things starting feeling too ordinary, Ryan would manufacture drama: fire the band on stage in Kansas City or play two shows as an acoustic duo but then refuse to play the third one. I suspected that was at least partially the reason why he was making time with Jenni. Flirting with the bass player while her punk icon kinda-sorta boyfriend drank in the back lounge? That's drama. Maybe not drama to the level of Fleetwood Mac circa *Rumors*, but enough to keep Ryan nourished.

Volatile as the new lineup seemed, Ryan was excited about it. He talked a lot about how Phil was an asshole he was thrilled to be rid of. He said that the new ensemble felt like a band instead of like people who happened to be on stage together. As he'd told a reporter before the Irving Plaza show, the goal on this tour was to lose the hit-or-miss reputation the band had built. "We'd rather hit every night," he said, mentioning that on previous tours, "on the nights we missed, it was usually an event because we were all so loaded. Mainly me."

And there were many nights where the new lineup hit hard. Like in Minneapolis, where we played the 7th Street Entry, the small club attached to the larger venue First Avenue, where the performance scenes from Prince's *Purple Rain* were filmed. We did the small room early, and then later the big room, Wilco played a set. As in New York, when Ryan was on his game because the Old 97's were in the building, the presence of Jeff Tweedy and Wilco kept Whiskeytown on point. Wilco was perched at the very top of that alt-country totem pole, and watching them from out in the crowd that night, I was confused by the worshipful awe with which the diehards regarded Tweedy. I thought he was a good songwriter, but Ryan was infinitely better. When Tweedy sang "Misunderstood," the true believers went glassy-eyed and slack-jawed, like Jesus was delivering the Sermon on the Mount. Between songs, when he stood at the mic, it was like the scene from *Forrest Gump*, when, after three years of running, Forrest finally stops in the middle of a desert road with a group of followers on his tail. "Quiet, quiet," one of the followers says to the others. "He's going to say something." Still, later in the set, when Tweedy called out Ryan from the stage, it felt good, redeeming, like Ryan had been sanctified.

A few days later, on November 5, Ryan celebrated his twenty-third birthday. In England, November 5 is known as Guy Fawkes Night, named for another rebel who liked to explode stuff. Ryan spent his birthday not plotting to blow up Parliament, but with a gig at the Omaha Ranch Bowl, which was both a bowling alley and a concert venue. Ryan got superdrunk, but he stayed in a good mood. He smiled for most of the show. He spent a whole song hilariously imitating Keith Richards's stage moves. They played such a long set that the house had to unplug the PA to shut the show down. The birthday boy wasn't going to be stopped by a lack of power. He grabbed his acoustic and played five or six more songs solo, with no mics or amplification. This was Ryan at his charming, charismatic best.

But as the tour wound through the Midwest that autumn, shows like Minneapolis and Omaha were the exceptions. Most of the sets were pitifully short. Back in Austin, when the new lineup was supposed to be rehearsing, they spent too much time drinking and screwing around, not enough time learning songs. The same thing that had happened when Mike Daly joined the band. Ryan had no interest in playing old tunes over and over to get the new people up to speed. So now they only knew about forty-five minutes worth of material. Forty-five was standard length for an opening set, but on this tour, Whiskeytown was the headlining act, contractually obligated to play sixty to seventy-five minutes. Instead they'd knock out forty or so, say goodnight, and then head back the bus to drink and chain-smoke. I worried that the Silver Eagle was too much fun, that they were ending the shows early just so they could resume the party in the back lounge.

Night after night, when I settled up with the promoter, I'd get bitched out because the set was about half as long as we'd promised. We were playing bars on this tour. And bars are not really in the business of hosting bands; they're in the business of selling drinks. It's just like with television: a program like *Friends* is the bait that brings in the audience, but the real goal is to sell advertising slots. When a band plays a small club, whatever happens on stage is the bait. The business is what happens behind the bar. If the band ends early, the crowd clears out early, and the promoter's angry because the register take is low.

Because of the short sets, the promoters were mad and the audience members were disappointed. Fans know to expect seventy-five to ninety minutes from a headliner. On that tour there were nights when the opening band—either Citizen's Utilities or the Volebeats—played longer than Whiskeytown did.

The other problem during these dates was that Ryan wouldn't turn down his guitar amp, no matter how many times JC the soundman begged him to. These bars had maybe three-hundred-person capacities, and Ryan was playing through this souped-up hundred-watt Fender Twin Reverb. The amp was so loud, it drowned out the vocals, Caitlin's fiddle, Ed's guitar, and even Jenni's bass. What these shows lacked in length, they more than made up for in volume.

"You're killing me," JC would tell Ryan. "Out front it sounds like shit."

But Ryan wouldn't turn down. So Ed would turn up. Then Jenni would turn up. Then Ryan would twist his knob another notch to the right. It was like a turtle race: every instrument slowly crept up and up until the band sounded like 130 decibels of crap.

About a month into the tour, we did a show in Fayetteville, Arkansas. The band played a supershort set, like maybe thirty-five minutes, and then walked off. The promoter was pissed. This was a Saturday night, and his bar was empty three hours before last call. "You screwed me over," he said when I went to settle up with him. "No way I'm giving you your guarantee."

The dude had a point. Our guarantee was $1,500. I could understand why he'd be angry about paying us nearly fifty bucks a minute. But my job was to get the money—no matter the set length or the sound quality. I don't remember what I said, but somehow I convinced him to pay me the full amount.

Out in the parking lot, I ran into Jenni. "You guys are gonna have to start playing longer," I said, "or I won't be able to get us paid.

And if you *can't* play longer, then I don't know. Maybe we'll have to put a different lineup together."

A little while later, Ryan came up to me. "Jenni's really upset about what you said." Apparently, she thought I was angling to get her kicked out of the band. I wasn't. I was just trying to squeeze five more songs out of them.

"All right," I said to Ryan. "Let's have a meeting."

So while the bus was still parked at the club, we got together in the front lounge.

"Listen," I said. "This is a headlining tour. These people are expecting you to play like seventy-five minutes." I told them they couldn't do a half-hour set and expect me to collect the guarantee. And I reminded them that the guarantee was a big part of what paid for touring expenses. "I got you this bus," I said. "So now you have all this extra time. You guys have a sound check every single day. That's an hour right there. There's no excuse."

They nodded and promised to play longer.

We may have been on a bus for this run of dates, but that didn't mean we were getting fat on porterhouses and pinot noir. The budget I had drawn up was tight, and in order to save money, the nine of us (six band members, two crew guys, and me) were essentially living on the Silver Eagle, whose interior square footage was small enough to make the engineers at Ikea sweat. Most mornings I'd roll out of my bunk to find the ashtrays littered with butts and the trashcans piled with bottles. Once a week, maybe, we'd treat ourselves to an extra hotel room so we could all grab a shower, but most days Uncle Donnie was the only one of us who got a room. The bus was our home, but it was pretty much the most unwholesome, dysfunctional home possible. A dive bar on wheels.

That night in Fayetteville, we kept the bus parked at the venue until 6:00 a.m. The next show was in Little Rock, and if we left right after load-out, we'd get to the hotel too early. Uncle Donnie would be sitting around the lobby for six hours, waiting to check into his room. So we waited, and when the sky lightened in the east, Uncle Donnie pulled out of the lot. We drained our beers, finished our cigarettes, and crawled up to our sleeping berths.

A couple hours later, JC woke up. He'd felt the bus rocking—not from side to side, but, strangely, from front to back. He climbed down from his berth to see what was going on. Uncle Donnie was revving the engine, shifting from drive to reverse to drive again, gunning it in both directions like he was stuck in a snow bank. But there was no snow in North Arkansas that November. Uncle Donnie had grounded the bus on a set of train tracks. He'd driven over a railroad crossing, and the underside of the bus had bottomed out on the hump of the tracks. Now a piece of the rear suspension was caught between the railroad tie and the track itself. The bus was physically connected to the tracks, and it would not come loose. Working the transmission shifter and the gas pedals, Uncle Donnie was going to force it loose.

JC looked out the window and could tell that the tracks were active. A train could come by any minute. "Uncle Donnie," he said, "shouldn't we wake everybody up and get 'em out of here?"

"Nah, son." Uncle Donnie rocked the transmission. "Don't bother. I almost got it."

While the rest of us slept unaware, JC looked at the driver and then down the tracks, listening the whole time for a train whistle. Uncle Donnie rocked us back and forth, back and forth. JC was just about to say, "Fuck this," and wake us all up, when Uncle Donnie floored it. With the awful sound of ripping metal, the bus broke free, leaving a piece of the undercarriage back on the tracks. The rest of us only found out about this when we woke up in Little Rock. For several days after that, the bus made a creaking sound from the rear suspension.

In the month we'd been riding the Silver Eagle, I'd learned that Uncle Donnie was the kind of guy you might call "colorful." One morning, when Donnie, Ryan, and I were sitting down at Shoney's, the bus driver ordered eggs Benedict. "And darlin'," he said to the waitress, "on the hash browns can you pour some extra 'holiday' sauce?"

A few days into the tour, he tried to con me—which shouldn't have been a surprise given that five minutes after I met him, he bragged to me that he'd conned the last tour manager he'd worked with. On the day it was my turn to be scammed, he'd just fueled up at a truck stop, and he was standing in line at the register, waiting to pay. He didn't know that I was standing a few people behind him. When he got to the counter, I heard him say, "Darlin', can you get me a blank fuel receipt?"

Pretty standard grift. He was going to forge a fake receipt for diesel fuel he hadn't bought, hoping to get reimbursed for money he hadn't spent. When you're tour-managing two or three buses, you can easily tell if one driver is slipping in extra receipts, trying to skim a couple hundred bucks here and there. You just compare his receipts against the receipts of the other drivers. But with only one bus, it's hard to double-check. If I hadn't heard him ask for the blank, the scam probably would have worked.

"Uncle Donnie," I said, turning my palms up. "I'm standing right behind you."

He shrugged, tucking his wallet into his pants. "Sorry, son."

Uncle Donnie liked to brag that the Silver Eagle was equipped with a diesel tank motor. I wasn't sure what that meant, other than he could get the bus moving really freaking fast. The sooner he got to the next town, the sooner he could go to sleep or head to a bar or whatever. So he always drove like he was being chased. Up front on the dash, he kept three devices: a police scanner, a radar detector, and a radar jammer. He also had a giant plastic mug that I suspected was filled with coffee and Baileys Irish Cream. The dude would drive so fast, we could barely walk around the back lounge. Standing up was like surfing—or like floating in zero gravity. The ground disappeared so quickly underneath you, it was like there was no ground at all. We were all drunk and dizzy, holding tight to whatever solid surface we could find. I should have fired him, but back then I was so green, I didn't know that you *could* fire the driver.

One night, when we seemed to be about halfway between yesterday's gig and tomorrow's hotel, we pulled into the parking lot of a Holiday Inn. I was confused. Why were we stopping early? Using the phone that rang from the back lounge to the driver, I called up to the front. "Uncle Donnie, why are stopping?"

"Son," he said, "we're here."

I looked at my watch. He'd driven four hundred miles in four hours.

As the tour wound back toward the Southeast, the band started taking longer sound checks, and they learned a few more songs. The sets never quite hit the seventy-five-minute mark, but at least the headliners could now do a solid hour.

Waiting to Derail

On a Saturday in Athens, Georgia, we played the 40 Watt Club, and my ignorance of college sports bit me in the ass. Because we only needed one or two hotel rooms per night, I usually made the reservations just a day ahead of time, which had always worked out fine. But then we showed up in Athens on the same day the Georgia Bulldogs were hosting the Auburn Tigers. Every hotel within an hour radius was sold out. Uncle Donnie needed to sleep, football game or no football game, but the closest hotel with vacancies was all the way in South Carolina. So during the afternoon, while everybody else slept on the bus, I rented a car and drove Uncle Donnie sixty miles to his bed.

On the ride across the border, he said, "Son, you're wearing me out today. But I know how you can make it up to me." He told me that when we got to Charlotte next week, he wanted to stay in a specific hotel he knew about, one that sat right next to a "titty bar" (his words). "You put me up in that place," he said, "and we're even."

So a week later, I was standing in the lobby of the titty bar hotel, checking in Uncle Donnie. Ryan had never been to a sleeze-motel like this, so he came along out of curiosity. The room was about twenty-five dollars more per night then we usually spent, but I wanted to make it up to Uncle Donnie for the Athens botch, so I splurged. I handed the clerk a hundred-dollar bill, and he handed me the key. Ryan, Uncle Donnie, and I walked to the room. When we opened the door, the first thing we saw was the bed. Heart-shaped, naturally. The TV was already switched on, tuned to the hardest in hardcore porn. The XXX equivalent of Swedish Death Metal. In front of the TV sat a couch stained with body fluids beyond contemplation. The room smelled like funk and sweat and cum, like syphilis was blowing from the HVAC system.

Ryan and I had never seen anything like it. We looked at each other, horrified. But Uncle Donnie dropped right to the couch and made himself at home. "Boys," he said, spreading his arms across the backrest, "when you get to be my age, there ain't no crime in paying for a blow job."

The Uncle Donnie tour ended in Norfolk, Virginia. On the way there, as we were barreling down US 58, the bus suddenly slowed and then puttered to a stop. We were out of gas. On a Silver Eagle, the engine is in the rear, so Uncle Donnie walked to the back lounge to try to prime the motor. He removed the cover, leaving the guts of the bus as naked and exposed as the porn stars I'd seen on that hotel TV. As Uncle Donnie worked, Mike Daly walked up and stood over him. Mike Daly was a Jersey wiseass. Uncle Donnie was a Tennessee redneck. When they were around each other, they both reverted to stereotype. Mike Daly became a wiser-ass. Uncle Donnie's neck got two shades redder. Now, the Jersey utility man looked down at the driver, who was elbow deep in the bus motor, and said, "Hmm. So, that's the engine, huh?"

A few minutes later, a pickup pulled over, and the driver volunteered to take Uncle Donnie and me to a gas station, where Donnie bought six gallons of windshield wiper fluid. I was just about to tell him that dirty windows weren't our problem, when he walked back behind the building and dumped all the fluid out into the grass—E.P.A. regulations be damned. Now he had six empty jugs. He filled them all with diesel fuel, and we rode back and got the bus started.

So far that fall, we'd managed to avoid playing sports bars, so Ryan hadn't felt the need to mock sports fans from onstage, and there hadn't been a repeat of the East Lansing incident. Then we showed up at the venue in Norfolk. It wasn't an all-sports-all-the-time kind of place, but on this Monday night, the bar TVs were showing *Monday Night Football.* Denver vs. Oakland. During the loud parts of our set, this wasn't a problem. But during the heartfelt acoustic section, as Ryan was playing a quiet song all by himself, one of the teams scored, and the people watching TV cheered. There was no verbal outburst from Ryan. No "fuck yous" into the mic. He just stopped playing, took off his guitar, and smashed it to pieces. Show over.

Shortly after Norfolk, I rewrote the Whiskeytown tour rider (the rider, as you probably know, is the document specifying the brand of beer the act gets, the type of food, the color of M&Ms, etc.). From that day forward, our rider insisted that all TV sets in the venue be turned off. *It doesn't matter if it's the World Series, the Final Four, or the Super Bowl,* I wrote. *If Whiskeytown is performing, there must be no television. Period. This is not negotiable.*

The next day, when Uncle Donnie dropped us off in Raleigh, everything felt pretty good. We'd finished a tour without anyone quitting or getting fired. It was two days before Thanksgiving, and the next run of dates didn't start until mid-January. We'd been going full blast since late spring. Everybody was ready for a break.

CHAPTER

As he'd later tell the *Austin American-Statesman,* "I live in places the way Tom Waits lives in places," so *home* for Ryan was far more temporary than for most people. Six weeks earlier, just before the Uncle Donnie tour started, Ryan had theoretically moved to Austin. But now, even though most of his belongings were sitting at Jenni Sperandeo's place in Texas, he decided to stay in Raleigh to get some writing and recording done. For the immediate future, Ryan would stay with me and Stephanie (whom Ryan called the Queen of Punk, a nod to that fact that she'd gone 100 percent new wave in her teenage years), sleeping in our extra bedroom.

Our house was on West Lane Street, between campus and the Capitol building, just off the Hillsborough strip. As the weather turned colder and the holidays approached, Ryan would walk from our place to Hillsborough and back. He came and went on his own, wrote a shit-ton of songs. Everything felt, dare I say it, normal.

And to complete the picture of domestic bliss, Stephanie and I went and bought a dog, Lucy, to go along with our cat, Little Kitty, whom Ryan loved. It was all as perfect as a Norman Rockwell painting—if you add beer and cigarettes.

One sunny Saturday, when we were all hanging out around the house, Little Kitty got out. This was a problem. She was about a year old and hadn't yet been spayed. So Ryan, Stephanie, and I went searching through the neighborhood, up, down, and around Glenwood Avenue, which today boasts a bunch of bars and restaurants but was fairly desolate back then. It took about an hour, but one of us eventually found her. Back in the house, with Little Kitty safe and sound, the three of us sat in the kitchen smoking cigarettes.

"God, I hope Little Kitty didn't get pregnant," Stephanie said. One rock star, one dog, and one cat made for fine additions to our family. We didn't need a whole litter.

Ryan puffed on his Marlboro and said, "If she did, at least you won't have to deal with the kittens for another nine months."

I wasn't sure I'd heard him right. "Dude," I said. "Are you fucking kidding me?"

"What do you mean?" he said.

"*People* take nine months to have babies. Cats take *two* months."

"What?" He looked at me like I'd just told him the Earth was flat. "Are you sure about that?"

Young Ryan thought every mammal took nine months to grow. It was one of those mundane little facts he was totally ignorant about. Because, really, why would Ryan need to know about feline gestation? Two months, nine months, who gives a shit? His brain was busy with more important work.

One night I was staying up late watching TV, when Ryan walked into the house. I asked him what he'd been up to.

"Just having some beers," he said. He reached into his pocket and pulled out a bar napkin with some words scribbled on it. "Let me show you this song I wrote."

He grabbed a guitar, and he played this magical, holy-shit-I-can't-believe-it sort of tune. He's always so great, so heartfelt, when it's just him and an acoustic.

"Goddamn, dude," I said. "That song's amazing. When did you write that?"

He put the guitar down. "Tonight."

"I thought you were at the bar."

He nodded. "Yeah, that's where I was."

Wait a minute. Something didn't add up. "You wrote the song while you were drinking at the bar?" I picked up the acoustic. "What guitar did you play?"

"I didn't," he said. "I just played the guitar in my brain."

I was dumbfounded. This kid could sit there drinking beer and scrawling lyrics, and while one side of his brain was singing the song, the other side was strumming along on an imaginary guitar. And he could do this so well, that back at my house he could pick up a real guitar and play the song perfectly the first time through? Flawlessly covering a tune that three minutes earlier only existed in his head? This wasn't songwriting; this was fucking *sorcery*. Dude was a warlock.

I'd worked with a handful of bands at this point, and I've worked with many more since. Bands with gold records. Bands with Grammy awards. I assure you, this is not normally how songs get written. Nobody writes with such ease and frequency. Now that I was living with Ryan, getting an up-close look at his process, the only explanation I could think of for his productivity was that he had longer antennae than anyone. The songs were already floating in the atmosphere, and he detected them before everybody else. Tunes got beamed down into his head one after another. His job was to jot down the lyrics and internalize the melodies as soon as they hit him. His job was to catch the lightning.

That Christmas, Stephanie and I threw a party at our house. The band came, along with a bunch of our Raleigh friends. Phil Wandscher even showed up, and he and Ryan got along just fine. It was really fun for all of us to get together away from the usual context, away from the bars and truck stops and hotels. There was no tension at all.

Ryan was in a really good place that night—that whole holiday season, really. Writing a lot. Recording a lot. Teaching himself how to play piano. He was as happy as I'd ever seen him. *Strangers Almanac* had been out for five months, and though it wasn't the commercial smash Outpost had been hoping for, the album had definitely moved well: approaching fifty thousand copies sold. Whiskeytown was now a hipster band of choice. Definitely on the way up. If you were a fan of Steve Earle, Wilco, and the whole *No Depression*/Americana scene, you knew about Ryan Adams—and his reputation for being equal parts talented and temperamental. He hadn't become the alt-country Kurt Cobain, taking y'alternative into the mainstream—but nobody else had, either. The genre remained where it had been a year earlier: lots of ink but no crossover success to show for it.

Much of the alt-country press coverage was devoted specifically to Ryan and Whiskeytown. The pieces that focused on the band's volatile and inconsistent live shows sometimes slanted negative, like the *Detroit Free Press* article from October that described them as "half band, half soap-opera." But reviews of the studio record were uniformly positive. In the 1997 edition of the *Village Voice's* "Pazz and Jop" poll of 441 American music critics, *Strangers Almanac* was listed as the 23rd-most-heralded album of the year, making it the second-highest-ranked alt-country record, trailing only Steve Earle's *El Corazon* at number eleven (Bob Dylan's *Time Out of Mind* topped the list, but because Dylan is legendary enough to qualify as his own musical genre, I'm not counting him as alt-country). To better appreciate how significant Whiskeytown's #23 ranking was, here's a partial list of alt-country artists who released albums in 1997 that *didn't* make the "Pazz and Jop" poll: Son Volt, Blue Mountain, Old 97's, 6-String Drag, the Backsliders, Hazeldine, Big Back 40, and the Supersuckers.

Ryan wasn't paying attention to album sales or critical acclaim. He was cranking out songs. He sat in my living room, playing me one great new tune after another, and I was learning that this was what got Ryan most excited: bringing a song into the world. The instant the inspiration hit him—*that* was the absolute best moment for Ryan. If he played the new song for you right then, you were lucky. Because the next time you saw him, he'd have written ten newer tunes, and you'd never hear that first one again. From that moment of inspiration forward, a song's grip on him would slowly loosen until, finally, it could no longer hold his attention. He'd have moved on.

"I'm usually about four or five steps ahead of myself," Adams told *The State* back in November. "You know how sometimes little kids, when they walk on their shadows, try to walk on their head? That's what I'm always doing."

Or as one of my buddies once said, "You can tell Ryan's losing interest in the song even as he's writing the song. That's why the lyrics in his first verses are always better than his second verses."

Waiting to Derail

By the end of 1997, Ryan had long before lost interest in the songs on *Strangers Almanac*. He had a backlog of new material burning a hole in his pocket. So a couple weeks before our Christmas party, he decided on a whim to go into a Raleigh studio. The goal was to complete a whole new record, from start to finish, in just a few days. Mixed, mastered, artwork, everything. Then, with no warning, he'd turn it in to Outpost. *Bam*. New album.

Chris Stamey from the dB's produced the new recordings. He also played bass, sitting in for Jenni Snyder, whose ability, he and Ryan agreed, wasn't up to studio snuff. Stamey invited Ben Folds to come in and play piano. Other than that, the lineup was the same as on the last tour: Caitlin, Skillet, Mike Daly, and Ed Crawford. They worked quickly, churning out a whole record in what felt like a long weekend.

Back at my house, Ryan picked some photos out of my collection, added them to a few pictures he'd taken, and then—sitting on the floor with Lucy the puppy nipping at the photographs—he used glue sticks and tape to paste together a cover for the album, which was titled *Forever Valentine*. Later we went to Kinko's and made ten or fifteen copies of the CD and artwork, dropping one into a FedEx envelope addressed to Mark Williams at Outpost. A musical Valentine's Day present from Whiskeytown, xoxo.

The band was still knee-deep in the *Strangers Almanac* touring cycle, so there was no way Outpost was going to release a new disc anytime soon. In fact, it never did get an official release, though the tracks "Don't Wanna Know Why" and "Easy Hearts" would later appear on the *Pneumonia* record. Still, *Forever Valentine* was important because it established early that Ryan was going to write and record songs on his own schedule. He wasn't going to shackle himself to the slow pace that the major labels had settled into by the nineties, where artists released a new record only after two years had passed since the last album. According to the prevailing wisdom at the time, you didn't want a band's second album competing against that same band's first album. But Ryan—always the student of rock history—wanted to do it seventies-style, when bands like KISS and Cheap Trick were cranking out a new record every nine months. "I think it'd be great to make a couple of records a year," he told the *Albuquerque Journal* shortly after finishing *Forever Valentine*. "It used to be like that. Dylan and the Stones and other bands put out lots of records."

Now that Ryan was living with me, I had a couch-row seat for his creative process. And I was learning that in terms of sheer output, he was flirting with Prince-level productivity. For as long as the band held together, the rest of us—musicians, crew, all of us—would be busy just trying to keep up with him.

CHAPTER

10

In mid-January of 1998, we left on a six-week run that would send us out to the West Coast. This stretch of shows would take us back to many of the cities we'd hit the previous summer on the RV tour, but now we knew the gigs were going to be much more crowded. Instead of playing to 150 people in a half-empty bar, we'd be playing to three hundred in a bar that had a line stretching around the corner. Instead of playing to a couple hundred in a small theater, we'd be playing for five or six hundred. Sometimes even a thousand. Heading west out of Raleigh that January, we were propelled by one other piece of adrenaline-spiking news: five days into the tour, Whiskeytown would be taping an episode of PBS's iconic *Austin City Limits*. It would be the band's debut television appearance.

The lineup and crew were the same as on the Uncle Donnie tour, with one notable exception: Uncle Donnie himself. Over the holidays, I received a call from Four Seasons Coaches, the company he drove for. The owner of the company told me that on the Silver

Eagle they had installed a computer that measured the engine's RPMs. "Uncle Donnie was either driving in first gear the whole time," the owner said, "or he was averaging almost a hundred miles an hour." The owner already knew the correct answer: B. So the company was going to make it up to me, he said, by giving us a new driver and a nicer bus. Now we were pointed southwest in a deluxe Van Hool with a pristine interior, including a shower with more pressure than those in many of the Super 8s we'd stayed in.

After an uneventful show in Houston ("uneventful" in a good way, like when the plane doesn't crash and all that happens is you get to your destination alive), we played Bryan, Texas. At the end of the show, as the band were walking offstage, Jenni's foot got tangled in Ryan's guitar cable, and she inadvertently knocked over Ryan's black Les Paul Custom, breaking the headstock off the neck. She felt horrible. She'd only been in the band for three months, and now she'd accidentally gone Pete Townshend on the frontman's first-string guitar—four days before the *Austin City Limits* taping.

Ryan sat in the Val Hool, staring down at the Les Paul's broken neck. He looked ready to cry. This was his favorite guitar. "What are we gonna do?" he said.

"Don't worry," I said. "This is not a problem. Happens to Les Pauls all the time." I told him we'd just mail the guitar to a luthier in Raleigh to be glued back together. After the fix, Ryan would never know the difference. In the meantime, we'd go buy a new one.

So the next afternoon, we sound-checked at Trees in Dallas, and then Ryan and I took a taxi out to the Guitar Center by the Galleria Mall. He sampled a bunch of different models, eventually deciding on a midseventies sunburst Les Paul. Perfect. Time to settle up and head back to the venue for the show. But walking up to the checkout counter, I realized that I'd left my wallet on the bus, which was still parked at the club. In my pocket was enough cash for the cab ride, but nowhere near enough to cover a $1,750 Les Paul. And there was no way we'd have time to taxi back to the bus, then back to the store, then back to Trees before showtime.

One possible escape hatch: I could recite my American Express number as easily as I could sing the ABCs. But without the card itself, and without any identification, what reputable big-box store was going to let me walk with a guitar that cost more than my first car? Now I was the one who might start crying. I told the sales clerk our situation: *Whiskeytown, major-label band, touring behind* Strangers Almanac, *playing at Trees tonight then off to Austin to tape* ACL. I don't know what part of that story resonated with him, but here's what happened: I gave the guy my AmEx number, he called it in, and the purchase was approved. No card. No ID. No matter. We loaded the new guitar into the cab and raced back to the club.

Ryan played the show superdrunk that night, but he was superdrunk teetering behind a sparkling Les Paul. Rockstardom has its privileges.

The next day, our new driver, Tim, steered us toward Texas's capital city, where we'd be playing a Saturday night show at Liberty Lunch, a tune-up for Monday's *Austin City Limits* set. These days *ACL* is recorded downtown, in the glittering Moody Theater, but back in the nineties, the show was still being produced on the University of Texas campus, in Studio 6A of Communications Building B, which, despite its Communist Bloc-sounding name and architecture, had become a legendary broadcast/performance venue in the twenty-plus years since *ACL* began taping there.

As we loaded-in that Monday afternoon, Ryan was nervous. Maybe it was because this was television almighty, a much bigger beast than simply banging out tunes for drunks in a bar. Maybe it was because of the legendary footsteps he and Whiskeytown would be walking in. Buck Owens and BB King. Townes Van Zandt and Stevie Ray Vaughn. Willie Nelson, Johnny Cash, and Merle Haggard. They all had stood on the *ACL* soundstage. Or maybe he was on edge because this would be another encounter with Rhett Miller and his Old 97's. Both bands would appear in the episode. A few days before the taping, Ryan was still talking trash about his Dallas-based "rivals," but because Miller was refusing to volley the insults back, Ryan's smack talk was losing some of its spirit. The cat had retracted his claws. "The only reason they're playing is because we're letting 'em," he told the *Fort Worth Star-Telegram*, following with, "I'm just kidding, you know."

It turned out that Ryan didn't face his unrequited rivals in Studio 6A that day. Each band's set was recorded at a different time in front of a different audience. The video engineers stitched the performances together in postproduction for broadcast. I don't even remember running into Miller and the Old 97's.

What I do remember is that Whiskeytown was as good as I'd ever seen them. They opened with the single "16 Days," Ryan plucking away at the new sunburst Les Paul, Ed Crawford bending the twangy licks that complemented Ryan's Byrds-esque jangle-picking. After a few measures, Caitlin joined in on the fiddle, and I could tell that her entrance made the audience edge forward in their seats. These fans, many of whom had surely skipped work to be here on a Monday afternoon, were alt-country true believers. If Whiskeytown's name and reputation hadn't already hooked them, the bittersweet tone of Caitlin's fiddle sure had. Then she joined Ryan in harmony on the opening vocal lines. Several audience members started clapping. Ryan and Caitlin singing together: the sound of Whiskeytown.

Dressed in blue jeans and a suit jacket, Ryan was taking his songs as seriously as the *ACL* audience was. On this day, he'd decided to care. And they loved him for it. In between tunes, he was charming and self-deprecating, setting up jokes that Caitlin would knock down. Their back-and-forth reminded me of Johnny Carson and Ed McMahon, and the Austin audience was just as appreciative of the Ryan/Caitlin banter as the *Tonight Show*'s Burbank audience had been of Johnny and Ed's.

During the quiet parts of the tight, twenty-five-minute set, the crowd stayed hushed with the same kind of reverence I'd seen superfans bestow upon Jeff Tweedy and Wilco a few months earlier in Minneapolis. During the loud parts of the set—all through "Yesterday's News," for example—heads bobbed like at a full-on rock show. Whiskeytown was *crushing*.

I'd been working with Ryan for eight months, and I had no doubt whatsoever about his artistic brilliance. I'd also seen his productivity firsthand. But a couple of weeks earlier, on a rainy Raleigh Sunday, I witnessed his range.

We were hanging around the house, kind of bored, when Ryan said, "Hey, man. Call Skillet, and let's go to the practice place."

All afternoon, the three of us drank beer and hung out and made up silly punk songs: Ryan on guitar and vocals, Skillet on drums, me playing bass. After we'd knocked around a half-dozen tunes, we broke for cigarettes. We drank and laughed about how good this ad hoc band was. Now the band needed a name. I knew Ryan loved cats, so I said, "How about Catbox?" I could already imagine the t-shirt: black, with a steaming litter box on the front. "But our first order of business," I said, "is to write Catbox a hit."

[125]

Ryan snubbed out his Marlboro. "What are you talking about?"

This was early 1998, and alternative rock was still king. "We need a radio single," I said. "Something that sounds like the Foo Fighters or the Stone Temple Pilots."

Ryan nodded, picked up his guitar. "Give me the name of the song."

I thought for about five seconds. "I Don't Wanna Be Like You," I said. It was the first thing that came to mind.

He put his finger on his forehead and then looked at his feet. After about four seconds, he pulled his finger away, raised his eyes to me, and said, "I got it."

He played the whole song from start to finish, writing the chord progression and lyrics on the fly. It just flowed right out of him. Then we played it as a band, with me tweaking the arrangement for maximum radio impact. Now it sounded a little like the Foo Fighters' "Monkeywrench." After playing it through a second time, all I could do was laugh. "I Don't Wanna Be Like You" was maybe five minutes old. And if we had recorded it that day, Catbox would have gotten a record deal. I know it.

The song was good, but it was more than good. It was a flawless rendition of a certain *kind* of song: alt-rock hit circa 1998. This was a different genre from Ryan's usual territory, and yet he'd mastered it. The kid was a genius at mimicry. By listening to a bunch of great songs, he'd taught himself to be a great songwriter—across all genres. If he wanted to, he could pen a perfect disco tune or R&B jam or probably even a Gregorian chant. Ryan hates new country, but if he were so inclined, he could set up shop in Nashville, crank out a bunch of tunes about pickups and dirt roads, and be a billionaire. But again: Ryan was never motivated by money. And like Dylan, Springsteen, Prince, Ray Davies, and all prolific songwriters, Ryan was much more concerned with writing something good than with writing something original. The best songwriters are all copyists to some degree. They don't get overly hung up on the fact that the tune they're working on might sound like somebody else's.

In fact, as Ryan was doing with "Monkeywrench" that day at Catbox practice, they often try specifically to craft a song in the style of another writer. They see it as a challenge. Moreover, they consider copying to be part of their education, a necessary step on the path to finding their own unique voice. Maybe it's not copying. Maybe it's stealing. Although he may have borrowed the idea from the poet T.S. Eliot, Picasso is widely quoted as saying, "Good artists copy. Great artists steal." The quote is probably apocryphal, but it makes a good point. When you copy something, the goal is simple duplication, which can be a valuable lesson in and of itself. You ape the techniques of another artist in an effort to master those techniques. But when you steal something, you bag it up and take it home with the intention of *making it your own*. As soon as it's yours, you're free to do with it what you want. Rearrange it. Break it. Spray paint over it. Picasso himself experimented in a range of established styles (Realism, Symbolism, Post-Impressionism) and took inspiration from other painters he admired (Gauguin, Matisse, Munch, Cezanne), but he eventually rearranged the techniques he'd stolen and molded them into Cubism, *his* style.

As we drove away from the *Austin City Limits* taping that day, I knew that at twenty-three, Ryan was already a good artist. He could copy better than anybody I'd ever met. And I suspected he was ultimately, like Picasso, not just a copyist but a thief. A great one. Still I worried he'd shoot himself in the foot long before his own artistic vision would have a chance to blossom. As brilliant as the *ACL* set was, to me it was just as bittersweet as the sound of Caitlin's fiddle.

Because it confirmed what I had begun to suspect: in order for Ryan and Whiskeytown to be world-beaters, all Ryan had to do was give a shit. Unfortunately, on lots of nights that was too much to ask.

After Austin, we were off to Albuquerque, then Santa Fe, then Flagstaff, where the state legislature had just passed a law making it illegal for bar employees to drink alcohol while at work. The promoter told me about the new statute as we were loading into the club that afternoon. Because it was January and the law had just gone into effect, the club was struggling with how to interpret the words "bar employees." For now, the dude was casting as wide a net as possible. "The minute your guys get up there and start playing," he said, "they instantly become employees of the club. That means no drinking on-stage." With his empty hand he yanked on an imaginary kill switch. "Or I shut the show down."

This was a problem. Whiskeytown not being able to drink on-stage was like Keith Richards not being allowed to smoke. Or Liberace not allowed to light candles. Ryan was pissed. He threatened to cancel. But the rest of us talked him into going through with it. Before the show he sat in the dressing room, stewing in his indignation. On-stage, drinkless and pouting, he treated the crowd to a minidiatribe about the unfair treatment the band had suffered at the hands of local and state authorities. Then, about twenty minutes into the set, he threw down his guitar and stormed out the back door, leaving everybody else onstage to shrug in apology.

As Caitlin and the band settled into the dressing room, I looked out to the crowd of about two hundred; they were visibly making the shift from confusion to anger. Then I saw the promoter holding the box filled with all the cash the club had collected at the door. If Ryan didn't come back soon and restart the set, this dude was going to abscond with the moneybox. I knew it.

"Don't take your eyes off that promoter," I told Ace, who was selling merch. "I'm going to find Ryan."

He wasn't on the bus. He wasn't in the back alley. I walked outside the front door of the club and looked both ways down the street. About a block away I saw the neon sign of what was obviously an old-man bar. That was the place. I opened the door and there he was, Ryan and four or five lizard-skinned drunks, sitting at the bar, sipping on Budweiser. "I'm not doing it," he said.

"You just played for twenty minutes and ran out the door," I said. "These people are going to want their money back."

"I'm not doing it. No fucking way."

I tried to think about which particular key would unlock the guy and get him to change his mind. Then I remembered that a few days earlier we'd talked about how expensive it was to paint a tour bus. "Ryan," I said, "right now we have the only bus in downtown Flagstaff. We're going to be awfully easy to find."

"What do you mean?"

"When some pissed off fan runs a key down the side of that bus, it's going to cost us a shitload to get it fixed."

For some reason that resonated with him. We walked back to the club together, and after what had amounted to a thirty-minute delay, Whiskeytown finished the show. Of course, half the crowd had gone home by then. Still: we got paid and got out of town.

The reviews from that tour were all over the place. One writer would say how magical a given show was—and the next writer the next show, how terrible. After solid gigs in Tucson and Tempe, at we arrived in Los Angeles, where on a night off Ryan got plastered while shmoozing with a Universal Music Group rep named Andy Nelson.

Well past midnight, after Andy dropped him off at Le Rêve—our West Hollywood hotel—Ryan stumbled up to the rooftop pool where some of the band members and I were hanging out. He kept tripping over lounge chairs and falling down to the concrete. I was worried we were going to have to fish him out of the pool.

I told him to come down to the room Ace and I were sharing. That way we could keep an eye on him in a confined and relatively padded space. The room was on the first floor, so Ryan and I took the elevator to the lobby. Walking past the front desk, I started to say something to him but then realized I could no longer see him in my peripheral vision. I turned around and saw that he had snuck behind the front desk, which was unstaffed for the moment, and he had grabbed the handsets of two corded phones. He put a handset up to each ear so that he looked like a set of parentheses (or an eighties-era stockbroker), and he shouted into both of them, "I'll have a bacon double cheeseburger with no mayonnaise and an extra side of bacon."

He was walking and talking, stretching the phone cords tighter and tighter until finally they couldn't stretch any further. Ryan let go and they sling-shotted back toward the desk, where they landed at the feet of the hotel clerk, who had just returned to his post.

The clerk bent over to pick up the phones. "That was not funny, sir," he said.

Walking into the room, Ryan's babbling woke up Ace, so the three of us went out to the patio to get some fresh air. The room was set a half-story below ground level, like an "English basement" apartment in a brownstone. So standing there on the patio, the three of us had to look up to see the street. Ryan reached into his pocket and pulled out a flask-sized bottle of Jim Beam. After finishing it off, he climbed up a small hill to ground level, where from behind the bushes, he fired the empty bottle toward Cynthia Street. It smashed in front of an approaching Honda Civic. The driver slammed the brakes. Ryan fell into the bushes and got mud all over his clothes. We dragged him down the hill and into our room before he got his ass kicked or arrested or both.

"Are the cops gonna get me?" he said as he climbed onto Ace's bed, covered in mud.

"Not if you shut the fuck up," I said.

He crawled under the covers and passed out.

At the Troubadour the next night, while I was onstage fixing something, Ryan pointed at me and then said to the whole crowd, "This is the guy that keeps our shit together. Give him a hand." The audience clapped, which felt nice, but they had no idea just how *not* together Ryan's shit was.

The Troubadour show was fantastic, but the following night's show at the Casbah in San Diego was so mediocre that Mark Williams from Outpost said to me, "If I had seen Whiskeytown play live *before* I heard their music, I never would have signed them."

That dud in San Diego was followed by really good gigs in Northern California, including a sold-out show at Slim's in San Francisco. The next day, we played Cotati, near Sonoma State University, at a place called the Inn of the Beginning. A tall, beautiful woman named Miranda worked there. Ryan was immediately smitten. "I want her to read me my Miranda rights," he said.

That afternoon, he and Ed visited a music store, where Ryan picked up a banjo and started shredding like a bluegrass Yngwie Malmsteen. "Wow, man," Ed said. "When did you learn to play the banjo?"

"I didn't," he said. "I just mess around on one whenever I'm in a music store."

He was teaching himself to play banjo one store visit at a time, just as I'd seen him teach himself to play piano. The guy was a natural, a wonderboy. But like Roy Hobbs from *The Natural*, as talented as Ryan was, he was cursed with a self-defeating hubris. Swinging for the fences only works if you make contact. The *Sacramento Bee* that week wrote that Ryan was "fast gaining a reputation as one of the most reckless figures in nineties rock."

"I sort of enjoy it, don't I?" Ryan told the paper. "I would much rather experience intense, beautiful life by experimenting and not limiting myself and not caring about what other people are thinking about the choices I make. I'm not saying everybody has to be unconservative with their lives, just that I'm not. I'm a wreck."

Steven Terry,
Chris Laney,
Phil Wandscher,
Thomas O'Keefe,
Caitlin Cary, and
Ryan (L to R) near
Bend, Oregon.
RV Tour –
September 1997
Photo courtesy of
Thomas O'Keefe

Chris Laney and
Caitlin Cary.
RV Tour – August
1997
Photo by Thomas
O'Keefe

Phil Wandscher
during the record-
ing of *Strangers
Almanac*.
Photo courtesy of
Chris Roldan

A drawing of Thomas by Ryan (note the cig and the Diet Coke). 1997
Photo by Thomas O'Keefe

Ryan at Niagara Falls, Ontario.
RV Tour – August 1997
Photo by Thomas O'Keefe

Ryan's guitar picks, featuring the Charlie Whistlenut sign-off.
Photo by Thomas O'Keefe

Mike Daly, Ryan, Alejandro Escovedo, Chris Laney, and Steven Terry
(L to R) in Seattle a week before the infamous Kansas City breakup.
RV Tour – 1997
Photo Courtesy of Chris Laney

Phil on the RV Tour
Near Joshua Tree, California
Summer 1997
Photo by Chris Laney

The amp that destroyed a dozen shows:
Ryan's Fender Twin Reverb, used from 1997 to 2000.
Photo by Thomas O'Keefe

The shirt says it all.
Photo by Thomas O'Keefe

Chris Roldan and Jenni Sperandeo.
Austin, 1997
Photo courtesy of Chris Roldan

Rehearsal for Whiskeytown Mark II –
Ed, Skillet, Caitlin, and Ryan
(L to R).
Austin – October 1997
Photo by Jenni Renshaw

Ryan pretends to drive Uncle
Donnie's Silver Eagle
(note Donnie's large "coffee" cup).
Somewhere in the Southeast –
October 1997
Photo by Thomas O'Keefe

Front of Whiskeytown tour laminate, featuring Thomas.
Photo by Thomas O'Keefe

Back of Whiskeytown tour laminate, featuring a Ryan Adams self-portrait.
Photo by Thomas O'Keefe

Ace making friends.
Middleton, Wisconsin – 1998
Photo by Thomas O'Keefe

Jenni and Caitlin.
Fall 1997
Photo courtesy of
Jenni Renshaw

Ed and Skillet unwind on the bus.
Fall 1997
Photo courtesy of Jenni Renshaw

Whiskeytown Mark II
Radio interview in New York City with legendary DJ Vin Scelsa.
October 1997
Photo courtesy of Jenni Renshaw

Jenni and Uncle Donnie NOT on the titty bar hotel sofa.
Fall 1997
Photo courtesy of Jenni Renshaw

Ryan does some housecleaning.
Uncle Donnie's bus – Fall 1997
Photo courtesy of Jenni Renshaw

Ryan in his hotel room, with necessary supplies.
Spring 1998
Photo by Jeff Caler

Stephanie O'Keefe tells Ryan what's what.
Backstage at Tramps in NYC
Spring 1998
Photo by Thomas O'Keefe

Big Ben. Parliament.
Mike Daly on a day off in
London – Spring 1998
Photo by Thomas O'Keefe

"The Kids." James Iha (Smashing
Pumpkins) and Ryan Adams.
The Borderline – London 1998
Photo by Thomas O'Keefe

Ryan, Dino Sex (GG Allin's drummer), and Thomas.
The Caboose, Garner, North Carolina – 1998
Photo courtesy of Thomas O'Keefe

Typical underwhelming audience for Whiskeytown on the Fogerty Tour.
Summer 1998
Photo by Jeff Caler

Ryan and Thomas on a London pay phone acting stupid (or normal).
Spring 1998
Photo courtesy of Thomas O'Keefe

The monkey glasses.
Fall 1998
Photo by Thomas O'Keefe

The Mikes have a beer.
Mike Daly and Mike Santoro
London – Spring 1998
Photo courtesy of Thomas O'Keefe

About to take the stage at Radio City Music Hall. Ryan, Danny Kurtz, Mike Daly (seated), Caitlin, Jon Wurster, Brad Rice (L to R).
July 1998
Photo by Thomas O'Keefe Courtesy of SleepyD

Ryan rehearsing with 7M3 in Thomas's Durham, North Carolina, living room. Ryan performed with 7M3 the next day in Raleigh. Jason Pollock, Jason Ross, and Ryan (L to R).
Photo by Stephanie O'Keefe

Ryan's 1974 Les Paul Custom. Bought in Dallas, smashed in Charlotte, featured on the tour shirt below, now residing in Thomas's garage.
Photo by Thomas O'Keefe

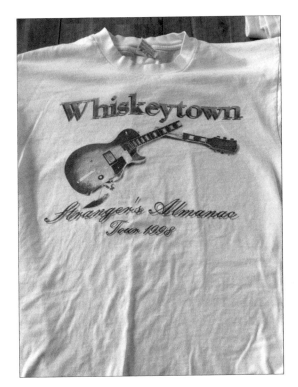

The shirt sold on the Fogerty Tour. Summer 1998
Photo by Thomas O'Keefe

Thomas's crappy Honda parked in front of Dreamland Studios.
Hurley, New York – Early 1999
Photo by Thomas O'Keefe

Ryan and Amy's Avenue A apartment.
New York City – Spring 1999
Photo by Thomas O'Keefe

The newlyweds. Skillet and Caitlin at their wedding. Raleigh – October 2000
Photo by Stephanie O'Keefe

Thomas and Mandy Moore.
Summer 1999 – opening for 'N SYNC
Photo Courtesy of Thomas O'Keefe

Ryan gets out of the tux as fast as possible.
Thomas and Stephanie's Wedding – Blowing Rock, North Carolina
Oct 2, 1999
Photo by Pat Moser

CHAPTER

11

A week after the San Francisco show, the wreck exploded. It was a Friday night in Seattle, Friday the 13th to be exact. We were playing the Showbox, which is right downtown, across 1st Avenue from Pike Place Market. The Showbox is one of those iconic old clubs that just about every touring act has hit at some point, from Duke Ellington to the Ramones to Snoop Dogg, and as you walk through the Art Deco interior, under the chandeliers and around the funnel-shaped columns, you can smell some of the sixty-years'-worth of beer and bleach that's been spilled since the place first opened in 1939. The venue seats a thousand people, and on that Friday night it was sold out, packed tight as the salmon sitting on ice in the fish stalls across the street.

After sound check, Ryan disappeared. I don't know where he went or what he did—maybe he settled in to another old-man bar, maybe he had some sort of drug connection in town—but when he finally appeared at the gig, he was completely messed up. He staggered around the dressing room, out of his mind on pills or booze. Maybe a combination of the two. Mary Lou Lord was the opening act, and after she said goodnight, we had about a half hour to get our gear ready and then get Ryan up onstage. But Ryan was still babbling, banging into things. Then, just when we were supposed to be starting our set, the fire marshal showed up with a clicker and a clipboard to make sure the venue wasn't over capacity. The place was that crowded. The good news was that the occupancy inspection gave Caitlin and me an extra fifteen minutes to tell Ryan to get his shit together.

After the fire marshal gave us the all-clear, the band took the stage, the crowd went nuts, and everything was fine. Almost. My eight months with the band had taught me that there were four distinct kinds of Whiskeytown show. There was the *So Incredibly Great It Changed Your Life* set, like at *Austin City Limits*, which happened maybe 10 percent of the time. There was the *Half-Baked Effort*, which was about 60 percent. Then there was the *Super-Punk Smash a Bunch of Shit* show, which was maybe 15 percent. The other 15 percent of the gigs were *Beyond Drunk*. Before the band had finished the opening song, I knew *Beyond Drunk* was what we'd be dealing with that night.

Ryan fumbled through a few tunes, singing maybe half the words, barely bothering to fret the Les Paul. I was standing next to the stage, down on the floor at crowd level, where I'd set up the guitar-tech station. As he was playing—or, more accurately, *not* playing—Ryan kept turning away from the audience toward me, signaling for my attention. "Dude!" he yelled down to me, over the noise of the band. "Dude, look!"

I figured he'd broken a string or knocked his guitar out of tune, so I got his back-up ready. But Ryan shook me off with a laugh. "Look!" he shouted. Then he launched into his Keith Richards

[134]

imitation: swinging his guitar around, raising his strumming elbow up to chin height, spreading his legs almost wide enough to reach from Seattle to Tacoma.

He and I had always joked about the cool Keef moves, and now here Ryan was, spoofing the Rolling Stone in front of a sold-out crowd, laughing his ass off, and trying to bait me into cracking up with him. This routine had been funny back in Omaha, where the audience had been smaller and he'd been happy-drunk instead of shit-house-wasted. Nah, who am I kidding. Adams doing Richards was dead-on hilarious. Always. But in Seattle I didn't want him to see me laughing. I wasn't about to encourage him. I kept my head down, eyes trained on the guitar tuner.

In every Whiskeytown show, there were the usual stretches of uncomfortable silence (they still weren't using a set list). But that night at the Showbox, with Ryan standing there mute at the mic, staring off into the darkness and wobbling like he might fall to his ass at any second, the dead space between songs felt longer than the songs themselves. Caitlin, Skillet, and Mike Daly tried to smile along like this was all part of the plan, but after a few of these awkward pauses, it was clear to all of us—band, crew, and crowd—just how blasted Ryan was. During one brutally long gap he looked out over the audience, and instead of saying, "Hey, y'all. We're Whiskeytown" or "Thanks, Seattle. You guys are great" or whatever script most typical frontmen would follow, he leaned into the mic and said to the thousand people who'd paid good money to be there, "You guys suck."

From my spot down on the floor, I heard a few laughs—but only a few. The crowd mostly seemed baffled. Ryan wasn't yet famous, so he couldn't coast on the horsepower of his own celebrity. The Showbox was thick with trucker hats and jean jackets, Pabst t-shirts and muttonchops. Seattle was *No Depression*'s hometown, and these were the devoted faithful. They didn't seem quite in tune with Ryan's punk rock sensibilities. They probably didn't know that Ryan dug Johnny Thunders, a junkie who would badmouth his audience in a good-natured way: "Why don't you kids take something?" Thunders would slur between songs, "You're boring me." On this night, Ryan *had* apparently taken something, and instead of warming up to the middle-finger-flying spirit of the set—the way Johnny Thunders fans would, or fans of the Replacements—this crowd seemed to be asking one another, "Why is this drunk asshole messing everything up?"

After one song, Ryan reached into his pocket and pulled out a Marlboro. But he was too far gone to notice that he'd put the cigarette in backwards: the business end was in his mouth and the filter was aiming at the audience. So of course he lit the filter, and of course it tasted like a chemical burn. Coughing out a *bleckh*, he threw the cigarette down to the stage. He looked over at Caitlin and then turned back to the crowd. "Caitlin's mad at me," he said, "'cause I'm all fucked up."

In their review of the show, the *Seattle Times* wrote: "Whiskeytown is one of the most promising of the new alternative country bands, but too many shows like the one Friday night at the Showbox and the North Carolina sextet may never live up to its potential. The group sounded ragged and tired, and there was too much wasted time in the short set. Long pauses between songs ruined the momentum, and there were silly, throwaway numbers, including a lengthy, unfunny reworking of 'Happy Birthday' for new singer guitarist Ed Crawford, and 'Laundry,' a childish parody of Neil Young's 'Helpless' with scatological references and lots of swear words."

The show finally wound down, and after settling up with the club, I corralled Ryan and everybody else and got them all out of there and onto the bus. We were headed back to the hotel, which was downtown, near the Space Needle and the Elephant Super Car Wash. But first we had to make a not-so-quick detour to the home of my wife's uncle, who happened to live in Seattle. The next day's show was in Vancouver, and I knew there was no way we'd clear the border crossing without first cleaning up the bus. So I had Tim maneuver the Van Hool up and down hills, squeezing through tight residential streets until we finally reached Stephanie's uncle's house, where we unloaded a bunch of the t-shirts (because we didn't want to pay customs duty on the merch) and stashed away all the pot (because we didn't want to end up in a Canadian jail). In a few days, after we crossed back into Washington state, we'd return to claim the swag and the weed.

By the time we got to the hotel, it was about 2:00 a.m., and Ryan was still wrecked—muttering nonsensically and nodding in and out. So Caitlin, Skillet, and I got him off the bus, and we started walking him around the block. It was closing time, and all the bars in the neighborhood were letting out. The sidewalk was littered with drunken stumblers. But Ryan was more than just drunk, he was drunk *plus*. Plus what? We couldn't be sure. And he wasn't just stumbling; despite our best efforts, he was falling. Leaning heavy into Skillet and me, Ryan would stagger along for half a block, and then his legs would go limp as cooked spaghetti and he'd smack the concrete. Then he'd garble something unintelligible, let out a laugh, and we'd pull him to his feet again. He fell down maybe five times before we finally gave up and loaded him back into the front lounge of the bus. Nothing we did was getting Ryan any closer to sober. Not water. Not coffee. Not the blunt force of the sidewalk. He'd babble for a minute or two, and then he'd seem to slide underwater, unconscious. A few minutes later he'd rise to the surface and start mumbling, and the cycle would repeat.

Now we were worried. We had no idea what exactly he'd drunk or what pills he'd taken, if anything. None of us were big into drugs, so we didn't know too-much-cocaine from too-many-painkillers. We weren't doctors or drug addicts—what were we supposed to do?

Mike Daly finally said, "Dude, my girlfriend's a pharmacy tech at Eckerd. Let's call her." We knew this was a desperate plan, but it was the best plan we had.

Mike Daly and I walked to a Denny's down the street to use the pay phone. By now it was about 4:00 a.m. on the West Coast. That made it 7:00 a.m. back in New York, where his girlfriend lived. I pulled out a calling card, he punched in the numbers, and we crossed our fingers she'd be awake, getting ready for her workday. Bingo. She answered and he explained the whole thing, but she didn't know any more than we did about how to revive a twenty-three-year-old fledgling rock star.

Walking back toward the bus, we were totally out of ideas. Then we saw our soundman headed our way.

"Hey, JC," I said. "You're going to Denny's, huh?"

He sucked on a cigarette. "Sure am."

"You gonna get you a Super Bird?" I said, talking about the famous Denny's turkey sandwich.

"Might," he said. "Might not." He looked back in the direction he'd come from. "By the way . . ." he took the cigarette out of his mouth nonchalantly as can be and said, ". . . the EMTs are on the bus right now. Trying to wake up Ryan."

I threw my cigarette down on the sidewalk, looked at Mike Daly, and said, "Let's fucking go."

The two of us took off running. When we came around the corner, there was the bus, flanked by two or three cop cars and an ambulance.

It turned out that soon after we'd left, Ryan had completely lost consciousness and hadn't resurfaced, so Caitlin or Skillet—one of them—found a different pay phone and called 911. I'm a little ashamed to say it, but my first thought after seeing the cops and EMTs wasn't concern for Ryan, it was *thank God we're playing Canada tomorrow.* On any other night, the back lounge would have been filled with marijuana smoke, dense as the smog in Beijing. The cops would have smelled it, and just as soon as they came down from their contact highs, they would have carted us off to jail. But tonight, because we'd already stashed the weed at Stephanie's uncle's place, there was nothing for the cops to smell but cigarettes and dirty laundry.

Soon the EMT was taking Ryan's blood pressure, and the seasoned veteran of the Seattle PD was telling me he didn't want to trade jobs with me.

"He's gonna be fine tomorrow," the EMT said when he stepped off the bus. "A little sore from all the falling he did, but basically fine."

I exhaled a breath I didn't realize I'd been holding. Ryan Adams hadn't died on my watch.

On to Vancouver. We'd gotten rid of the weed, but who knew what else Ryan might be holding. Who knew what kind of mess he'd make of the border crossing. Who knew what kind of jibber-jabber he might say to the officers and immigration officials. He'd already suggested imprisoning President Clinton. Hopefully, he wouldn't recommend jail time for the Canadian Prime Minister.

CHAPTER
12

A week later, after Vancouver, Boise, and Salt Lake City, we woke up in Aspen. I walked off the bus and took in the scene. It was late February in the Rockies. Fat snowflakes fell on the pedestrian mall as shoppers walked in and out of quaint shops. The slope-lined Aspen Mountain made for a postcard-perfect backdrop.

Ryan stepped off the bus, bracing against the cold, looking like he hadn't showered in a week. He scanned the surroundings, tilting his chin toward the mountain, where the pines were dusted with snow and a chairlift wound its way skyward. Then his gaze caught on something, and his face turned as sour as month-old milk. "What the fuck are we doing in a ski town?"

"What do you mean?" I said.

He shook his head in disgust. "This is a ski town."

"Well, yeah," I said. I wasn't sure I understood him. Or maybe he was fucking with me. On the itinerary for that day it said *Aspen, Colorado*. Who on this earth doesn't know that Aspen, Colorado, is a ski town?

Waiting to Derail

Ryan Adams didn't know. It was one of those things he was strangely ignorant about. And as soon as he found out, he was pissed. "This is fucking bullshit," he said, retreating back inside the bus. "I can't believe we're doing this."

For Ryan, a ski town was like a sports bar, but worse. It was a sports bar expanded to town-size and filled exclusively with frat boys and yuppies. On the one hand, I saw his point. Aspen is probably the least punk town in America. But on the other hand, shut up and enjoy the scenery.

Plus the gig was sweet. In addition to our $1500 guarantee, the club was springing for three or four hotel rooms—on a Friday night in the height of ski season. We checked in to those rooms, and, having slept on the bus for too many nights in a row, I took maybe the best nap ever. At lunchtime, I awoke feeling great, hoping the extra sleep had improved Ryan's mood.

But on the walk over to the venue for load-in, he was still at it. "We're not a ski town band," he said. "I'm not doing it."

The club was called the Double Diamond, and the guy who managed it had gone to NC State. He was a bald guy, supernice, and we all felt the Raleigh kinship right away. Ryan went ahead with sound check, and everything seemed fine. I figured the ski-town issue was settled.

But then, on the walk back to the hotel after sound check, Ryan said, "Cancel the show. Tell that Raleigh dude I'm sick."

"He just saw you in person," I said. "He knows you're not sick."

"Cancel it," Ryan said. "I'm not doing it." He stamped the snow off his boots and walked into the hotel lobby. "I'm not doing it!"

Cut to three hours later. He was still repeating, "I'm not doing it." His needle was stuck in the groove. Leaving the hotel: "I'm not doing it." Trudging back to the club through the snow: "I'm not doing it."

I finally grabbed him by the shoulders. "Ryan, you have to do it," I said. "We've already taken the hotel rooms. We've already sound-checked. The dude knows you're not sick. Just power through it."

He broke away. "I'm not doing it." That's when I knew that the Double Diamond was going to be one of those nights where we were double fucked.

Whiskeytown took the stage, and there were about two hundred people in the club, including the actor Kevin Costner. Ryan sleepwalked through a couple tunes, and then after song number three, he twisted the volume knob on his amp—the hundred-watt Twin Reverb that JC had been battling for months—all the way to the right. The guitar was so loud, it overpowered the drums, the bass, the whole PA system. Then he hit a ferocious E chord: BAAAAANNNNNN. He stomped on his echoplex delay pedal and hit the big E a second time. Now the chord repeated in rapid-fire succession: BAANNN-BAANNN-BAANNN-BAANNN. Just when that got as annoying as you can imagine, he reached for the tuning knob on his E string and started unwinding it. The pitch dropped steadily lower and slower: BAANNN, BLLAAAAAAANNN, BLLLLAAAAAAAAAAAAAAANNN. The ugly fart noise swirled around the room like a bad acid trip. It sounded like Ralph Steadman had painted it.

At this point, Caitlin, Skillet, Mike Daly, Ed, and Jenni put down their instruments and walked off the stage, leaving Ryan out there alone with only the ever-descending, ever-repeating sonic nightmare to keep him company. With the noise still swirling, Ryan dropped to his knees and lay flat on his back. Center stage, horizontal, his guitar still blasting out his version of Lou Reed's *Metal Machine Music*. He stayed there flat, not for what *seemed* like twenty-five minutes, but for twenty-five long, literal minutes. I timed it.

JC and I stood at front of house, looking at each other like, "What do we do? Do we cut off the PA?"

Earlier that tour, Ryan had told a Phoenix newspaper, "I don't give a fuck about our audience. I just make the doughnuts. They eat 'em. I don't want to sound rude, but I can't be concerned with what they want, because I'm not doing it just for them, I'm doing it for me."

But this wasn't Ryan making art for Ryan. And it wasn't Ryan making doughnuts for an audience that may or may not appreciate them. This was Ryan doling out punishment. He was punishing me. Punishing the audience. Punishing the club that had committed the mortal sin of being located in the shadow of a ski resort.

Twenty-five minutes. Imagine what that must have felt like. Plop a three-year-old down in front of a piano and then set your watch for twenty-five minutes. Seventy-five percent of the crowd was now gone. You better believe Costner had bailed. The club was down to maybe fifty people. And then, without saying a word, Ryan stood up and started playing a song. A real song as opposed to John Cage-style performance art. The band left the bar and got back on stage. They played for forty-five more minutes and called it a night.

When it was time for me to settle up with the supernice bald guy from Raleigh, he was so furious, he wouldn't even look at me. We stood in his office, and he refused to make eye contact, even as I apologized. I stared at the top of his bald head as he looked down at his desk, angrily counting a stack of fifteen one-hundred-dollar bills.

Slapping them down. One hundred. Two hundred. He counted to fifteen and then dropped them into my open palm. I was about to back out the door, when I remembered the long walk from the stage to the bus. The cold, the snow, the ice.

"Hey," I said. "Can I get a couple of your guys to help us load the gear out?" His eyes finally met mine. He looked ready to fight. But in the end, four big dudes from the Double Diamond, dudes who'd had to work right through Ryan's racket—they probably could have filed an OSHA complaint—helped us lug and load equipment out to the bus, where Ryan sat in the front lounge cackling with laughter, telling everybody how the whole night had been hilarious.

The next night's show was at the Bluebird in Denver, and because it wasn't sold out, we'd agreed to do an in-studio performance that morning at Boulder's KBCO in an effort to move a few tickets. KBCO is the most influential AAA (adult album alternative) radio station in the United States. They essentially invented the format, which puts heavy emphasis on midtempo, singer-songwriter-based material. "16 Days" was a perfect fit for AAA stations, and making friends with the folks at KBCO would not only lead to more airplay in Colorado, it would likely snowball to other AAA stations across the country. Bottom line: scoring a live in-studio in KBCO's Studio C was a big deal. Much more was at stake than simply selling tickets to that night's Denver gig.

We got maybe three hours sleep on the drive from Aspen to Boulder. By the time we arrived at the station, it was about 8:00, and everybody was exhausted. Still, this should have been uneventful. Play two songs acoustic, just Ryan, Caitlin, and Mike Daly. Then plug the Bluebird show, make nice with the KBCO staff, and get out. Easy.

Ryan was still sleeping off the Aspen destructo set from the night before, so Ace, JC, and I loaded the gear into the studio and set everything up. Then, when everything was good-to-go, I woke up Ryan and brought him inside to meet the KBCO rep.

"Okay, everybody," the station guy said. He was very Birkenstocky, speaking in a voice dripping with Sleepytime tea. "We're all superexcited you're here today." He requested that one of the two songs be "16 Days"; that way the station could put a live, KBCO-exclusive version of the single into rotation. Once "16 Days" was out of the way, Ryan, Caitlin, and Mike Daly could play any other tune they wanted.

I worried that Ryan would choose "Don't You Wanna Smoke Some Crack with Me" as the second song, repeating his stunt from the Louisville station. That bit had been hilarious, but KBCO wasn't the place to risk upsetting anybody. The goal for today: just play nice.

Ryan had other plans. He decided that he wasn't going to play "16 Days." No way, no how.

"Why not, dude?" I said. We were standing in the studio, all the gear mic'd up and ready.

"I don't want to sing that song," he said.

It wasn't that he *couldn't* sing the song—like, for instance, because it was too early in the morning, he'd had too little sleep, and his voice wasn't ready. No, he could sing "16 Days," all right. He just didn't want to.

I relayed the bad news to the station rep.

"Bummer," he said, very friendly-like. "If you don't play that song, then we're not going to be able to air the session."

So I went back in the studio to talk to Ryan. "If you don't do the single, they're not putting us on the air. They're gonna tape the interview and then let it rot in a closet somewhere."

He shook his head. "I don't wanna do it."

"Then why are we wasting our time right now?" I said.

We went back and forth for about ten minutes. I'd beg the station to let the band not do "16 Days," the rep would refuse, and then I'd go beg Ryan *to* do "16 Days."

It was a standoff, and I felt like a UN negotiator. As usual with Ryan, I needed to find the key to the back entrance. What was the one thing I could say that would get him motivated to do what he needed to do? Carrot or stick? In Huntsville, it had been threatening to dump him on a Greyhound. In Flagstaff, it had been the potential cost of repainting a vandalized bus. But that morning in the KBCO studio, after having gone through the whole Aspen mess only hours before, I was exhausted. I had no energy left to solve the Ryan puzzle. So I opted for complete honesty.

"Listen," I said. "I'm tired. I know you're tired, too. We both want to go back to bed. Caitlin and Mike Daly want to go back to bed. And we can. We *can*. Just power through '16 Days.' Get it over with, and you're done. Ace and I will pack everything up. In fifteen minutes, you'll be asleep on the bus. Come on, man. Let's do this." I'd fired the best weapon I could think of.

Here's what Ryan said in return: "I don't have to kiss some guy's dick just because he wants to hear the single."

Well, as we should have guessed, the mics were hot. And our Birkenstock-Sleepytime buddy was sitting in the control room, listening to the whole thing. He walked into the studio and, with a calmness probably steeled by a thousand hours of transcendental meditation, said, "Why don't you guys get the fuck outta here."

Two weeks earlier, Ryan had told the Sacramento paper, "Because I have a devil-may-care attitude and won't grit my teeth and kiss ass, people keep saying: 'Man, you're throwing it all away.'

But if I quit this band today, I would get a job, come home, have a beer, have something to eat, and then sit down and play a beautiful song."

Now we were getting tossed out of the most important AAA station in America. As we climbed back on the bus, I had to hand it to Ryan. The songs meant everything to him; the career meant nothing. But he didn't realize—or didn't care—that so many other people's fortunes were connected to his. When he pissed down his leg, he splashed everyone else. No matter. He knew what was important to him, and he knew how to get it. I had promised him sleep in fifteen minutes. He was back in his berth fast asleep in five.

CHAPTER

13

The tour that took us to *Austin City Limits* and then out to the West Coast had started in January. Now in March, we had a much-needed two-week break at home. After everything that had happened out West—Ryan passing out on the bus in Seattle, the Aspen meltdown, the KBCO standoff—I needed to mentally prepare myself before heading back into battle. So I watched George C. Scott's opening speech from the movie *Patton* over and over, until I was ready to cut out the enemy's living guts and use them to grease the treads of our tanks. I was ready. Once more into the breach.

Just like that, we were back on the road, playing shows in the Midwest. Same romantically linked lineup, same sweet tour bus. This time, however, we were joined by a new soundman, Jeff Caler, and a new opener, Fastball, the Austin-based band who'd recently released their debut single "The Way." As Whiskeytown rode the glistening Van Hool from Minneapolis to Madison to Milwaukee, Fastball trailed behind in their beat-up, ten-plus-year-old van.

Waiting to Derail

For these dates, Ryan stopped drinking. Totally. Not a drop. I'm not sure exactly why. Maybe it was because he always seemed to be racing against his own mortality, pushing himself to be as creative and productive as possible for the finite number of days he had on this Earth. And maybe he finally realized he was wasting too much of that limited life span being messed up. On this tour, he whizzed around the bus like a hummingbird, staying up late gulping coffee and chain-smoking cigarettes, sleeping for maybe four hours, then waking up and doing it again. Because there was no alcohol *down* in his system to counterbalance all the *up*, a billion ideas flowed from him all at once, all equally urgent and important. It was relentless. Remember on *Beavis and Butt-Head*, how Beavis, after eating too much sugar or downing too many pills, would transform into his alter ego, the twitchy, erratic Cornholio? I still think of this run as the Cornholio Tour.

The shows were better for it. In a review of the Milwaukee gig, the *Journal Sentinel* wrote, "Whiskeytown seems to be this month's pick among college radio and underground press circles, but this time the hype is justified." Unlike so much of the band's recent press, there was no mention of drunkenness or sloppiness. Between Ryan's newfound sobriety and the fact that our driver, Tim, liked to listen to Amy Grant while motoring us around, from a distance we could have passed for a Christian rock act.

But only from *long* distance. Where Ryan was now lagging in the alcohol-intake department, Ed's drinking had become nearly biblical. Every day he'd wake up at lunchtime and hit the sauce. By sound check, he'd be not just buzzed, but wasted. After a nap on the bus, he'd start drinking again during the show, and then, afterwards, he'd keep pounding until 3:00 or 4:00 in the morning, when he'd pass out in the back lounge with a cigarette hanging from his mouth.

Meanwhile, the friendship between Ryan and Mike Daly was taking hold. Most days, while Ed and Jenni slept off their hangovers and while Caitlin and Skillet were out exploring whatever town we were in, Ryan and Mike Daly would be camped out in the front lounge, hopped up on truck-stop coffee, writing songs, and planning to take over the world.

On April Fools' Day, we were scheduled to play a sold-out show at the Paradise in Boston. Most of the band rode up to New England in the bus, but Ryan and Mike Daly were supposed to arrive later that afternoon by plane. Ryan's impatience with waiting around to play the gig had begun to outmuscle his fear of flying. This plan would allow them to spend a few extra hours in New York City, where Ryan was already starting to build a new life.

Two weeks earlier, Stephanie and I had bought a house, not in Raleigh but in Durham, which allowed her to be closer to her job at Mammoth Records in Carrboro. The place was in a neighborhood called Parkwood, a suburban area dotted with seventies-era ranch homes. Ryan was still crashing with us, but now, instead of being located stumbling distance from Raleigh's Hillsborough St. bars, the three of us were twenty miles out. Ryan was not happy about being extracted from his element. In the short run, though, it didn't matter because Whiskeytown was leaving North Carolina, heading straight back out on a run of dates that would deliver Ryan to his girlfriend Amy's Manhattan apartment, which had become his northern residence.

Up in Boston, load-in came and went with no word from the frontman and the utility man. Then sound check came and went. Still no word. Then, as Fastball was setting up for their check, my pager beeped. I returned the call. *We're at the airport. There's a huge thunderstorm. The flight is delayed.*

Waiting to Derail

Ryan and Mike Daly finally did board the plane, but as it taxied out to the runway, it was struck by lightning. It had to retreat back to the gate. A half hour before doors would open in Boston, I got a call from Ryan. He told me the story. I looked at my watch and asked him if they could catch another flight. "I'm not getting on a plane now," he said. "No way. I'm not doing it."

This was no surprise. Ryan was already a nervous flyer. The fact that he'd wanted to fly in the first place is testament to the gravitational pull of NYC and Amy. By this point, it didn't matter anyway. Even if Ryan agreed to catch a later flight, they'd never make it to the venue by showtime (or even an hour or two late—Axl Rose time). You couldn't do a Whiskeytown show without Ryan Adams; I had no choice but to cancel.

At ten minutes until doors, I found the promoter and Fastball's tour manager, and I told them what happened. There was a long line standing outside the venue on Commonwealth Avenue, waiting in the rain to get in. I knew I had to go out there and be honest with everybody.

"Sorry, guys," I said, walking up and down the line. "It's not happening. Ryan's stuck in New York. His plane got struck by lightning." A few people laughed. They thought I was telling an April Fools' joke. "I wish I *was* joking," I said. "Believe me."

Fastball ended up playing the show by themselves, doing a headline-length set. We didn't stick around to watch, but my guess is that most people in the crowd didn't mind. After all, Fastball's single, "The Way," was currently rocketing up *Billboard*'s Modern Rock Tracks chart. Ten days later, it would reach number one and stay there for seven weeks. Whiskeytown had the tour bus, but Fastball had the hit song. Many times over the next ten days, we'd be sitting in the back lounge, watching our opening band's video on MTV. Then we'd look out the bus window and see the same guys we'd just seen on our television screen following behind us in their van.

Strangers Almanac may not have generated a hit, but by the spring of 1998, lots of music people knew about Ryan and Whiskeytown. In Minneapolis, we met Bill Sullivan, longtime tour manager for the Replacements. He regaled Ryan with Paul Westerberg/Tommy Stinson stories. At Trax in Charlottesville, Dave Matthews walked up to me, asking if I could introduce him to Ryan. Dave was really humble and polite. Ryan liked him a lot. In New York, I introduced Ryan to Merle Allin and Dino Sex, two guys who were polar opposites of Dave Matthews, at the extreme other end of the polite spectrum. Merle Allin is the older brother of GG Allin, the notorious punk rocker who—before his death—had achieved a certain degree of underground fame for his onstage behavior, which included self-mutilation and onstage defecation. Merle played bass for GG. Dino Sex played drums. Ryan was superexcited to meet both of them.

In the late eighties, my band ANTiSEEN became friends with GG Allin. After gigging together a few times, we ended up making a record with him called *Murder Junkies*, and he started to enjoy visiting North Carolina from Boston, where he was living at the time. He liked hanging out with us, and he liked getting away from New England.

In those days, ANTiSEEN's singer Jeff Clayton and I were working at a place called Transworld X-Ray Corporation in Pineville, North Carolina, just south of Charlotte. We built X-ray machines. When you're in a touring band, you need a bullshit day job to pay the bills, and the job at Transworld was great because they never hassled us about the off days we needed. In July we got a whole week off, which we filled up with tour dates. It's not fat-bottomed girls that make the rockin' world go 'round; it's flexible day jobs.

One day, Jeff thought it would be funny to put together a video compilation of GG Allin's onstage shenanigans. So he made a twenty-minute-long VCR tape of some of the most disgusting stuff GG had ever done: shitting all over the stage and throwing it into the crowd, sticking a hot dog up a prostitute's ass and then eating it, swinging a real dead cat by the tail . . . GG's grossest greatest hits. Jeff took the tape into Transworld, and one of our coworkers asked if he could borrow it. Like 90 percent of the people we worked with, this guy was a redneck from South Carolina who drove across the border into Pineville to clock in at Transworld. Our work buddies weren't big city people. When they needed to go into Charlotte to run an errand, they'd hit up Jeff and me for directions.

"Goddamn, man," our coworkers said to Jeff the next day. "That shit's crazy." So the next guy down the line asked to borrow the tape. Then the next guy. After a month or two of the tape circulating, we were working with a hundred rednecks who all knew who GG Allin was. In this one way at least, these blue collar South Carolinians were more culturally aware than many of the Lower East Side slacker-kids crashing on mattresses on Avenues A, B, and C.

The holidays were approaching, and the Transworld Christmas party was scheduled to take place in the ballroom of the Hilton off Tyvola Road in Charlotte. This was the big once-a-year affair, where all the guys would bring in their wives to meet the boss, everybody gathering around the open bar, juggling drinks and appetizer plates, trying not to spill Bud Light on the one suit and tie they owned. Coincidentally, GG was going to be in town that night, so Jeff and I decided that we would bring him to the party.

We rented a stretch limousine and pulled up to the Hilton entrance. Jeff, me, our girlfriends, and GG climbed out of the limo and strutted into the lobby. We were wearing suits; GG was wearing dirty ripped jeans. We had ties around our necks; GG had a dog collar around his. The second we walked through the ballroom doors, there was a collective gasp. Everybody stopped and stared. The place went dead quiet. But the shock-and-awe wasn't because GG was dressed like GG. No, everybody fell silent because at Transworld X-Ray Corp. circa 1991, GG Allin was a huge fucking celebrity. This guy that so many of them had seen on their TV screens was now live in the flesh in the Hilton ballroom. It was the same gasp that Tom Cruise would have gotten. After a few beats, the drinking and socializing continued. I can still picture GG in his mirrored cop sunglasses, standing in line for a shrimp cocktail next to the owner of the company, flirting with the gaggle of secretaries that stood behind him. One of the redneck dudes walked up to GG and after chatting with him for a few minutes said, "You're pretty cool for a guy who eats shit."

Later that night, some of the Transworld partygoers took GG to a titty bar—maybe the same one that Uncle Donnie would patronize years later. At some point, he paid a stripper five bucks to piss into a glass. He sat at the bar with a beer in one hand and the stripper piss in the other. When the bouncers yelled out last call, GG guzzled one glass, then the other. The stripper piss was his nightcap.

The last gig on the Cornholio Tour was at the Variety Playhouse in Atlanta. Ryan was still sober, and he was superexcited that his friends from Birmingham-based Verbena had come to the show. Before going on that night, he walked into the dressing room, grabbed the two bottles of liquor that came with our rider, and emptied them both into the toilet, saying, "I am sick and fucking tired of playing in a band with a bunch of drunks!"

For a long time, Ryan had been the drunk everybody else was sick of. But now he'd trained his sights on Ed (a heavy drinker who was a seriously talented guitar player) and Jenni (a regular drinker who was only moderately talented on bass). In Ryan's mind, Jenni was guilty of being too mediocre; Ed was guilty of being too drunk. He was regularly missing sound checks. He was so wasted and obnoxious at the border crossing on the way to Toronto that the customs agents tore through the bus in retaliation.

Ed's drinking had been escalating for a while, but since the holidays, it had really amped up. He and Jenni lived about forty-five miles from downtown Raleigh, in a town called Mebane. On the night before Christmas Eve, he drove into Raleigh, and he and Ryan went out drinking on the strip. The next morning, Christmas Eve, Ryan's older brother Chris—who would pass away in 2017—came by my house to pick up Ryan and take him to Jacksonville to be with his family. But Ryan wasn't at my house. He was still out with Ed. Chris said he'd try back again in an hour. During that time, Stephanie made a few calls, found out where Ryan and Ed were, and brought them back to our place. It was 9:30 a.m., and they were absolutely bombed.

"Ryan, you get in there and take a shower right now," Stephanie said. When she spoke up, you listened. "You are not going to your mother's house stinking like somebody mopped the bar floor with you."

Ryan laughed and cut up and definitely did not take a shower. His brother returned and poured him into the car like pancake batter. They hit the road for Jacksonville.

"I gotta go home," Ed slurred, grabbing his keys. "But first we gotta find my car."

I took the keys from him. "There's no way I'm letting you drive anywhere."

After we found his car, I drove him back to Mebane in it. Ed passed out in the passenger seat. Stephanie followed behind us in her car. Ed and Jenni lived in an old country house with a driveway nearly as long as a football field. As we approached the place, I woke him up with an elbow.

"Hey," he said, wiping his eyes. "Can I drive up to the house? I don't want to show up in the passenger seat of my own car."

He wasn't going to kill anyone in his own driveway, so I said sure and pulled over. We got out of the car to switch seats. He gave me a sloppy hug. He was still wasted. He dropped into the driver's seat and looked back up to me. "I haven't even done any Christmas shopping yet," he said.

I watched him putter up the driveway, feeling horrible for him and Jenni. I knew that as soon as he walked into the house, he was going to pass out, sleep for twelve hours, and wake up to a no-present Christmas.

By the time Ryan was dumping the bourbon bottles into the toilet in Atlanta, Ed and Jenni's positions in the band were tenuous. One night on the Cornholio Tour, we'd all gone out to see the movie *Titanic*. And now, with Whiskeytown's first European tour set to start in two weeks, Ed and Jenni were about to hit the iceberg. They were too busy partying in the back lounge to notice.

Because Ed was a punk icon, firing him was a delicate task. The plan was to cut Jenni loose and then hope Ed would quit in protest. Once we got back to Raleigh, that's exactly what happened.

Waiting to Derail

Many years later, Jenni would tell me that one day she ran into Ryan in New York. Almost literally ran into him. She walked around a corner and bam, there he was. They practically chest-bumped.

"Oh, hey, Ryan," she said. "How you doing?" She told me he had no idea who she was. He looked at her and registered nothing. It had been a few years since she'd played on his stage and ridden his tour bus, but still. Without saying a thing, he kept on walking.

And that's why you might still see a musician in Raleigh wearing a shirt that reads: *I played in Whiskeytown and all I got was this lousy goddamn t-shirt!*

The European tour started in Stockholm, followed by Oslo, Malmö, and Copenhagen. For those first few days, everybody was excited and in a great mood, especially Mike Daly, who, after Ed's departure, had moved into the lead guitar slot. He always saw himself as more than just the utility man. I suspect that from the beginning, lead guitar was the job he really wanted. He was doubly happy because he'd brought in a buddy to play bass, a guy named Mike Santoro, who had played with him in the New Jersey band Swales.

This was Whiskeytown's first time across the pond, Ryan's first time applying for a passport. The State Department rejected his original passport photo because it didn't meet regulations: Ryan's hair was hanging down over his eyes, and it was hard to see his face. This failure to appease the bureaucracy threatened to sink the whole Europe trip before we even got off the ground, but luckily our travel agent—a guy named Robert Becker, who was an aspiring alt-country artist and had played piano on the big Gin Blossoms album—was able to get Ryan to a passport expediting office in New York for a last-minute application. In this second photo, Ryan went for function over fashion, and the government issued his passport.

Europe breathed new life into the band. Strange cities, strange languages, strange food. Strangely awesome liberal drug laws. The Copenhagen gig was inside Freetown Christiania, the hippie-squatter-village-cum-open-air-hash-market. From a distance, the vendors' tables didn't look so different from what you'd find at a farmer's market in the Catskills, except that everybody seemed to be selling fudge. As far as the eye could see: fudge for days. But it sure didn't smell like fudge. We weren't the only American band wandering through Freetown Christiania. At some point we saw Lenny Kravitz inspecting the merchandise. At least it looked like Kravitz through the fog of my contact high.

When you first head out on tour, everything is thrilling and chaotic. But soon, once you get rolling, it turns very methodical and repetitive. Even though you're in a different city every night, every day is essentially the same. Europe was no different. The novelty wore off quickly. After a back-straining bus and ferry ride to Glasgow, Ryan's mood darkened. He was super pissy and super bored. Plus he was drinking again. Cornholio, we hardly knew ye.

After the last show with Ed and Jenni in Atlanta, Ryan had gone back with me to my new house in Durham, far from the action of Hillsborough Street but only about ten miles from Chapel Hill. At that point, he was still off the sauce. One night he said, "Man, let's go to Chapel Hill and maybe have a beer."

We drove to a bar just off Franklin Street, and he drank one and only one Pilsner Urquell. We talked about the upcoming European tour, ran into a couple friends, everything was cool. Then we drove home and went to bed.

The next night he said, "Hey, man. You wanna go to that bar again?" So we went back to that same bar, and this time he drank exactly two Pilsner Urquells.

Waiting to Derail

On the drive home to Durham, we didn't say much. Both of us were staring through the headlights, listening to AM talk radio. After a while, he said, "Man, do you think I'm turning into an alcoholic?"

I looked at him. "What do you mean?"

"Last night I had one beer, and tonight I had two beers."

"All right."

He reached over and turned down the volume on the radio. "That's a one hundred percent increase."

I laughed. "If you ever turn into an alcoholic," I said, "you'll know it. That fact that you can go to a bar and only drink two beers means you're *not* one."

"Okay," he said, turning the radio back up. "Good."

I'd run into lots of legit drunks in my day, and Ryan wasn't one of them. To me he always seemed to be drinking mainly to fuel the image he'd created for himself, not because he had a serious problem.

Now, in Glasgow, he seemed to be hitting the bottle out of pure boredom. Whiskeytown—the band, these songs, these shows—no longer held his attention.

In the dressing room after the uninspired Glasgow show, Ryan announced to the rest of us that he was quitting the band. "I'm sick and tired of this," he said. "We're done." We'd heard this kind of thing before, of course, but unlike, say, Kansas City, this time Ryan wasn't kicking anybody else out. This time he was giving himself the boot.

We listened to him babble on, and we all argued and fought. And poor Mike Santoro—the new guy who was so excited just to be here—he'd played five measly shows, and now the whole thing might be disintegrating.

We eventually talked Ryan back from the ledge, and the band didn't break up that night. The real problem was that the dude had been out on tour for too long, almost exactly a year by that point. He could no longer concentrate on the shows. Mentally and creatively, he needed to move on to whatever came next.

In the short term, what came next was Manchester. Then, for the European tour finale, two sold-out gigs at the Borderline in London. The Borderline is where lots of American bands make their London debut, and these were big, high-profile shows. The band was superstoked. Even Ryan was jolted out of the doldrums. The day before the gig, we did a full round of radio and press. Mark Williams from Outpost flew in. Chris Roldan was there. James Iha from Smashing Pumpkins, who in a month would release their *Adore* album, showed up to hang out with Ryan. Earlier in 1998, Iha had put out a solo alt-country–influenced record that, like *Strangers Almanac*, was produced by Jim Scott. He was a supernice Midwestern dude, and he and Ryan were building a solid friendship.

Everybody was happy in London—for a while. The shows were stellar, a reminder of how fantastic Whiskeytown could be when Ryan gave it his all. The *Times* of London raved: "Adams seemed lower-key and more vulnerable than when I saw the band in February in Nashville, where he exuded a glamorous swagger that was one part Keith Richards, another Marc Bolan. But this was a tighter band performance that emphasized the tireless support of the fiddle player and second vocalist Caitlin Cary . . .. Whether they be drinking to remember or drinking to forget, Whiskeytown never fail to move the spirit."

But immediately after the shows, having "conquered" London, Ryan's malaise returned. He was ill-tempered with me and the band and uncooperative with Chris Roldan. Ryan was over this record. He was ready to go home and stay home. The record company, however, wanted to move more units. They wanted the tour to keep rolling. So less than a month after landing back on American soil, we'd be heading out on another run. These would be the band's most prominent dates yet, for the biggest crowds they'd ever played for, by far. A year earlier, when I started with Whiskeytown, we were doing neighborhood bars. Now we were about to do a month of twenty-thousand-seat amphitheaters, opening for a rock-and-roll titan: John Fogerty.

For most bands, getting the chance to share the stage with Creedence Clearwater Revival's main man would be the break of a lifetime. But most bands aren't fronted by Ryan Adams. None of us knew it yet, but that summer would mark the beginning of the end of Whiskeytown.

PART

3

YESTERDAY'S NEWS
(SUMMER 1998–SPRING 2000)

CHAPTER

14

On a tour poster, the Fogerty/Whiskeytown pairing looked perfect. Fogerty was the legend. Ryan was the promising upstart, a younger version of the famously cantankerous Fogerty, who, as the creative force behind Creedence Clearwater Revival, had been playing Americana music since long before the genre had that name. For years, however, Fogerty had refused to include the old CCR classics in his live sets because of an extended legal battle with Fantasy Records, the label that owned the publishing rights to the Creedence catalog. Fogerty and Fantasy had been fighting since 1970, but in 1988, the suits and countersuits reached the level of the absurd: the label sued the songwriter for stealing from himself. Not exactly, but essentially. Fantasy's claim was that Fogerty's solo song "The Old Man Down the Road" borrowed from his CCR song "Run Through the Jungle," a tune that the record company owned. Fogerty won the suit, and eventually—after the case went to the US Supreme Court—his legal fees were covered.

The point here is that it had been a long, long time since Fogerty had played CCR songs live. That was all going to change in the summer of 1998. His new live album, *Premonition*, featured Creedence's greatest hits, as would the corresponding amphitheater tour. Needless to say, with this kind of buzz, John Fogerty didn't need a support act. Tickets were going to move regardless of who opened. Adding Whiskeytown to the bill was a gift, like Mean Joe Green tossing his jersey to the youngster in the old Coke commercial. *Hey, kid. Catch.*

These were important shows, and they necessitated major changes in the lineup. In the weeks leading up to the Fogerty tour, Jacknife's Chris Roldan had long talks with Ryan about needing to improve the band's musicianship. Roldan knew firsthand that as the stakes got higher, the playing had to get better. Roldan had once been the drummer for a San Francisco outfit called the Himalayans, featuring a pre-Counting Crows Adam Duritz on lead vocals. While still in the Himalayans, Roldan cowrote the song "Round Here," which later became a hit on the Counting Crows' debut album, *August and Everything After.* But when the Himalayans transitioned to Counting Crows, Roldan lost his spot on the drums. The stakes had surpassed his talent. Now, as Whiskeytown's manager, he wanted to ensure that Ryan had major-league talent supporting his major-league songwriting ability.

To satisfy Roldan's request to step up the musicianship, Ryan tapped Brad Rice and Danny Kurtz from Raleigh's the Backsliders to play guitar and bass, respectively. The Backsliders' *Throwing Rocks at the Moon* had come out a year earlier to a lot of positive attention, so Brad and Danny were already prominent alt-country players in their own right. Their addition meant that Mike Daly was back to being the utility man and that his buddy Mike Santoro was out. Neither of the Mikes had messed up on the European tour; it's just that Brad and Danny were seasoned Triangle veterans, and Ryan liked the idea of getting the package deal from an established band. Still, Mike Daly's ego was bruised a little. His stint as lead guitarist had lasted just a few weeks.

The next move was the one Roldan had intimate experience with: upgrading the drummer. Skillet was a great guy and a good player, but he wasn't opening-for-John-freaking-Fogerty good. So he was replaced by Jon Wurster from Chapel Hill indie-icons Superchunk. Naturally, Skillet's absence disappointed Caitlin, but ever the professional, she soldiered on.

Wurster was a step up musicianship-wise, plus with Superchunk he'd been out on high-profile tours like Lollapalooza, so playing in front of an amphitheater-sized crowd wasn't going to faze him. He was far more experienced than any of us. Unbelievably kind and sweet-hearted, Wurster was like a drumming yogi. He was über-politically correct, but his political correctness ran much deeper than just using polite language. He genuinely cared about other people; he was fiercely empathetic. One time we stopped at a rest area so I could make a phone call, and Ryan kept honking the horn in a playful way, making it hard for me to talk over the noise. I knew he was just messing with me, and I didn't care. But Wurster was really angry with Ryan. When I got back in the van, Ryan said to him, "What are you so mad about?"

Wurster pointed out the windshield toward some tables sitting in the grass in the distance. "Those people," he said to Ryan, "they were having a nice picnic. And you disturbed them by beeping the horn."

A friend of mine called this new roster the Whiskeysliders. I think I prefer WhiskeySliderChunk, which sounds less like a band and more like an appetizer at Applebee's. The lineup might have been

Frankensteined together, but it was a juggernaut. Three days before the start of the Fogerty tour, they played an incredibly great warm-up gig at the Brewery. And as we headed toward Indianapolis for the first date, I was hoping that this summer—and this lineup—would jolt new life into Ryan, the band, and *Strangers Almanac*.

Pulling into the loading area at Deer Creek Amphitheatre, I was met by a phalanx of tour buses and semitrucks. Transporting a full-production amphitheater tour (a "shed" tour, as it's commonly known) requires a whole fleet of vehicles. For these dates I'd decided we didn't need a bus. Whiskeytown was back where we'd started: in a passenger van, pulling a trailer.

A few weeks earlier, while the new lineup was rehearsing in Raleigh, I sat everybody down and said, "This is going to sound crazy, but I think we should do this tour in a van." I knew that caging a volatile personality like Ryan in small confines for too long was a risk, but I was playing the long game. The tour started in the Midwest, and with all of us cooped up in a van, the first week would suck. But then we moved to the Northeast for three weeks. That's where we'd get the payoff. The money we saved by renting a cheap van instead of an expensive bus would allow us to hub out of New York for that three-week stretch. We'd leave Manhattan every morning, roll out to Poughkeepsie or Scranton or wherever, and head back to the City to spend the night. "It'll be a lot more fun this way," I said. "We can do this."

Ryan was sold. By now he had essentially moved out of my house in Durham and was living nearly full time at Amy's new apartment in the West Village. Staying in New York every night meant he'd be sleeping in his own bed. I figured some regular home cooking would temper the fact that he was flat-out sick of touring, John Fogerty or no John Fogerty.

But now in Indianapolis, as I struggled to back the trailer into the dock, I was wondering if my idea to forgo the Van Hool for these dates had been a mistake. When you're a baby band opening for a big name on a shed tour, the first day is like boot camp. The headliner's tour manager immediately dresses you down—especially if you're young, hot shit, and you show up in a van and trailer. These days, nearly twenty years later, I tour-manage the headliner, and with all the moving parts I'm trying to keep track of, the last thing I need is the opening band acting out of line. So on day one, I've got to set them straight. I've delivered the *Listen, Youngster. Here's How It's Going to Work* speech to support acts many times.

On the Fogerty tour, I was the youngster on the receiving end of the talking-to, courtesy of the production manager, a guy nicknamed Springo. "I don't wanna see your fucking band on *my* stage once you're finished playing," he said. "And I don't wanna see any of your guests backstage. If I ever do see your guests backstage, no more fucking passes for you. Zero. Done. You understand?"

I don't think he was poking me in the chest, but he might as well have been. He was an old-school dude, and that kind of intimidation was sport for him. Even though I was thirty-four, I was still the punk kid pulling up to the loading docks in a van and trailer, which is like bringing a slingshot to the shooting range.

On the fourth night, we were in Minneapolis getting ready to sound-check, when I heard Springo shouting at me. "Get in here, fuckhead!" I asked what he wanted. "Last night I saw your hammerhead singer. With some guest. On my stage."

The night before had been Summerfest, and I knew the person he was talking about: Mel from Milwaukee. She was our friend, but she *wasn't* our guest; she was a guest of either a radio station or one of the sponsors.

"Let me ask you a question, Springo." I knew I had the bastard nailed. "How many backstage passes did you give me last night?"

"Four!" he said. "I gave you four. I remember it!"

I reached into the back pocket of the same dirty shorts I'd been wearing for a week, and I pulled out four passes. "Here," I said, handing all four passes back to him. "I didn't have any guests last night. If my singer was on your stage, it's because he was with one of *your* guests."

I'd produced the evidence. He was busted. But he shook his head and said, "You and Hammerhead are still guilty by association."

I smiled and said, "Hey, man. Have a great day off tomorrow." From that moment forward Springo would call Ryan "Hammerhead." And I would retaliate by killing Springo with kindness.

"Fuck you," he said, throwing the four passes into the garbage can.

The next gig was at Pine Knob Amphitheatre, forty miles north of Detroit. After the show, we went back to the hotel, a new high-rise in the Detroit suburbs with a vast, open atrium that rose twelve or fifteen stories above the lobby. Ryan stayed up really late, getting shit-housed-drunk with Ace and our new soundman, Jeff Caler. Like on the European Tour, caffeinated Cornholio was dead; drunk-ass Ryan Adams was back. At some point, he walked out of the hotel room into the hallway, which opened to the atrium. From there he could lean his chin over the railing, peek twelve or so stories down, and see the lobby and common areas, all spruced up with indoor-friendly foliage. He looked over at Ace and said, "I can fly."

Ace laughed.

"No, really," Ryan said, wingspanning his arms wide. "I can fly! I can fly!" And, just to prove to Ace that he really could, he lifted his knee up to the railing.

The new lineup had played really well for the first few dates, and everybody had been on their best behavior. But boredom had begun to seep in. That's what happens when you're the opener on a shed tour. On the one hand, you're living the dream. You're in the top 1 percent of all bands. Sharing the stage with bona fide rock stars, playing for thousands of people, being treated to full catering, spreading out in a nice backstage area with showers and towels and cold beer and a deli tray with a pimento in every olive. Hard to complain about those conditions.

But on the other hand, you're spending twenty-three long hours a day getting ready to do a forty-five-minute set. Those forty-five minutes are great, but they fly by. Every hour you're not onstage, you're waiting. You show up at load-in, and you wait for sound check. Maybe you get one, maybe you don't. But either way, you gotta wait. Fogerty was a rigorous sound-check guy, a perfectionist. Every now and then, with an hour or so until doors, he'd take off his guitar and say, "That's good. Let's go eat dinner." And we'd have time to set up and sound check. But more often he'd check for two hours, playing the same song over and over, working on it until doors opened. We'd have to throw our gear up onstage while the crowd was filing in. No check at all. We had waited around all day for nothing.

On a shed tour, the opener goes on at like 7:45, when it's still daylight and most of the crowd is still outside in the parking lot slamming Bud Lights. The seats are nearly empty when you start.

Nobody's paying attention. They're spreading out their blankets and checking out the merch stands and bitching about how expensive beer is on the inside. By the time you say goodnight, the place is maybe half-full. Seven or eight thousand. And when they cheer, it's not because you rocked, but because you're *done*. Now nothing stands between the audience and the act they came to see. It's 8:30 p.m and your workday is already over. That leaves a long night left to kill.

I know these are first-world problems. None of this sucks that bad; all of it beats flipping burgers. But like with any job, after a while, you fall into a routine, and the routine can get monotonous, especially for someone with a short attention span like Ryan. He hated every bit of it. Touring had been hard enough for him when we were doing sold-out headlining shows. Even the novelty of our first tour of Europe barely held his attention; he only got fired up for the London shows. On the Fogerty tour, he slept a lot. He played guitar and wrote songs. He spent time dealing with an inner-ear cyst that was bothering him. He tried to power through the boredom, but the lack of stimulation was killing him. He'd never wanted to do the Fogerty tour in the first place. Chris Roldan and Jenni Sperandeo had pressured him into it.

To combat the touring drudgery, Ryan tried to manufacture action whenever he could. That's what he was up to at the hotel in Detroit, all blasted drunk, faking like he was going to do a half gainer from a twelve-story-high railing. "I can fly!"

Ace had no idea if Ryan was serious or not. Ryan was so unpredictable, so fucked up—and from time to time could seem so depressed—that maybe he was about to fling himself from twelve stories. Ace wasn't taking any chances. He grabbed Ryan by the waist and dragged him back into the room.

Once we got through that first week and started hubbing out of Manhattan, Ryan was much happier. I went to visit him and Amy in her new apartment on Christopher Street. It was above a gay bar called the Hangar, which to a North Carolina guy like me looked extrabondagey. Lots of the dudes who walked in and out of the Hangar could have played the part of Rob Halford in a Judas Priest tribute band. As Ryan and Amy showed me around their pad, they were so proud. And I was thrilled for them. It was a great setup.

Meanwhile, the rest of the band and crew (everybody except Mike Daly, who was at his place in Jersey) stayed at the Ameritania Hotel at 54th and Broadway, around the corner from the Ed Sullivan Theater, where David Letterman taped his show. As per the plan, we'd wake up, go get the van from the outdoor lot where I'd parked it, drive to whatever town we were playing, and then end the night back in New York.

The upside was all the time we got to spend in Manhattan. On off days, everybody would spread out and do their own thing. Ryan was home with Amy. Caitlin would read and take in the cultural sites. Wurster kept mostly to himself, working on a comedy project he was writing. Brad and Danny ran around together. Ace, Jeff Caler, and I would go down to the East Village to hang out with Jesse Malin and the D Gen guys, which would inevitably turn into a 4:00 a.m. bender at the rock club Coney Island High. Or we'd head to Lakeside Lounge, the bar on Avenue B that alt-country musician/ producer Eric "Roscoe" Ambel owned. (Ambel would later partner with Van Alston, owner of the Comet, to open a Raleigh location of Lakeside Lounge, which eventually became Slim's Downtown Tavern.) Across the street from the Ameritania was a bodega that became our one-stop shop for food, beer, and nearly everything else. One day when Brad was standing in line, Gene Simmons from KISS came in wearing black leather pants, a burgundy jacket, and snakeskin boots. The Demon bought a Diet Coke and a box of tampons.

The downside to all the New York awesomeness was the difficulty of getting everybody out of the city to play the shows. Inertia. That was the problem. Objects at rest staying at rest. Once Ryan was home on Christopher Street, he didn't want to leave. Every morning we'd have to beg him to get to the van. He would be late, and then I'd have to call and wake him up. "I don't want to do it," he'd say, pissed that Whiskeytown had been booked on the Fogerty tour in the first place.

But he had to do it. My job was to make him do it. Still, I was starting to agree with him that the off days were much more fun than the show days. By this point, a full year after *Strangers Almanac* had been released, it was clear that the record wasn't going to yield a hit song. Sales had slowed to nearly nothing, stuck near the fifty thousand mark. So every night at 7:45, the act that took the stage opening for Fogerty was a band with no hit, touring behind a stalled album that was a year old. Rock critics loved Whiskeytown, but Fogerty's audience couldn't care less. A similar dynamic had happened in 1989, when the Replacements opened for Tom Petty. Fogerty's crowd had bought tickets to see a legend. Whiskeytown was nothing but forty-five minutes of noise standing between them and CCR's greatest hits. When Ryan hit the stage with his mop of hair and his eyeliner, looking like he had been dipped in beer then crusted with cigarette ash, Fogerty fans didn't know what to make of him. They nodded politely for half a song and then took off for the concession stand.

Just to keep himself interested, Ryan started tanking the shows on purpose. He stopped even trying to win over the audience. The set featured so many new tunes, the band barely played anything from the album they were ostensibly touring to promote. Ryan was in full-on fuck-around mode. In the space between songs, he would freestyle cheesy covers. At the Hershey, Pennsylvania, show, he played most of the set with a towel over his head. When he talked into the mic, he was funny—but in a smartass way, saying things like, "Be sure you stick around for John Fogerty. He's from the swamps of California." Or "We're Whiskeytown, from the bayou of North Carolina."

I braced for Springo to tap me on the shoulder and say, "Hey, fuckhead. Tell Hammerhead to shut his fucking hole." But the tap never happened. Apparently, Springo was more concerned about guests on his stage than he was about Fogerty being mocked by the opener. The crowd noticed, though, and they found Ryan's banter less than hilarious. They had come to hear the hits, not to listen to a punk-ass kid crack jokes at a legend's expense.

After the show in Wallingford, Connecticut, Ryan went back to Manhattan while the rest of us stayed in New England, killing a day until the Boston show. The last time we'd tried a stunt like this, the plane was struck by lightning and Ryan never made it up to Boston. So I knew that letting Ryan spend the off day in New York was a gamble, but I was trying to keep him in good spirits. While the rest of us were eating seafood in Mystic, Ryan was back on Christopher Street.

On the morning of the Boston show, Ryan called Chris Roldan and told him he wanted to cancel. The ear cyst that was bothering him had flared up. It was painful. It was making him dizzy.

He said there was no way he could do the show. Of course, when I heard about Ryan wanting to cancel, my first thought was that the New York inertia had struck again. Now that he was home, he didn't want to leave.

Thirteen years later, Ryan would publicly admit to suffering from Ménière's disease, an inner-ear disorder that causes vertigo and dizziness. He'd say that flashing lights—be they stage lights or flash photography—make the vertigo even worse. Ménière's is a degenerative condition, so back in 1998, were we witnessing the onset of the disease?

I don't know for sure, not even now. What I knew then was this: Ryan was demanding that Roldan cancel Boston. Wanting to cancel was nothing new for Ryan, but this time, because of the cyst, he could point to a tangible medical condition.

Roldan wasn't buying it. He tried to talk Ryan into going through with the show, just as I had so many times before.

"Why don't we pretend for one minute that *I'm* the *artist*," Ryan said to him, "and *you* are the *manager*."

Ryan won. We canceled. It was the second time we'd axed a Boston show in three months. Even though Ryan got his way, that didn't change how frustrated he was with Jacknife for talking him into doing the Fogerty tour in the first place. The next day, Wednesday, July 1, he decided he'd had enough. He officially fired Chris Roldan and Jenni Sperandeo.

Months later, when they were sitting around a table with their attorneys, negotiating the terms of their separation, Ryan would say to Chris and Jenni, "You did *nothing* for me," which is ridiculous. They were among Ryan's first supporters. They championed him from the beginning, doing everything they could to help him become the musician who would bring alt-country to the mainstream. They gave Ryan the opportunity to succeed or fail on his own terms. It wasn't their fault that he was so self-destructive. You can take a horse to water, but you can't keep him from drinking 'till he pisses everybody off and passes out.

Chris later told me a story about something that happened just before I'd gotten that first call to tour-manage Whiskeytown. At that point, he and Jenni were really concerned about Ryan. They thought he might die—maybe from an overdose, maybe drunk in a gutter. Because they didn't yet have me or anybody else in Raleigh who could help look after Ryan, they called his mother in Jacksonville. She said, You know, Chris, Ryan is going to do whatever he wants to do. No matter what. You can't stop him. Then she gave Chris an example. She said that when Ryan was twelve or thirteen, she took him to the orthodontist to get him braces. After a few weeks, he decided that he was done with them. He said to his mom, Take me back to get these braces taken off. And she said, No, Ryan. We paid for these. You have to keep them on. She turned away, thinking that the discussion was over. But then, a while later, she walked into the garage, and there was Ryan, standing in front of a mirror, mouth open. He was holding a pair of pliers. And all by himself, by hand, he was pulling the braces out of his mouth.

Even as a young kid, his determination was astounding. But even more astounding was his willingness to execute that determination. He wanted those braces gone. They were soon gone.

So I became Whiskeytown's manager. By default, I suppose. With Jacknife out, the band needed somebody to help make the big-picture decisions and to oversee the relationships between Ryan and the record company and between the band and the booking agent. I had never managed an artist before—certainly not one at the major-label level—but given that I'd been by Ryan's side for over a year, I guess I was as qualified as anybody. Much of the team (the label, the agent, the attorney, the touring outfit) was in place, so in the short run my job was just to keep doing what I'd been doing.

The next Fogerty show was at Radio City Music Hall. Everybody, including Ryan, was fired up to be there. And the Whiskeytown set was great. Because it mattered. Like at the Borderline in London, the prominence of the venue snapped Ryan out of his tedium. At Radio City, he gave a shit. But it wouldn't last.

Three days later, we were all standing in front of the Ameritania, waiting for Ryan to show up for the drive to Saratoga Springs. We were used to him being late, but not this late. I called Amy's apartment from a pay phone. No answer. I called again. And again. Finally I caught a cab and rode from Times Square down to the West Village and stood near the entrance to the Hangar, at the door that led to the upstairs apartments. It was locked. So I waited until some other tenant of the building happened to come home. When they unlocked the door, I slid inside. I walked up to Amy's unit and pounded and pounded until Ryan finally answered, looking just as ragged as the very first time I'd come to his Raleigh apartment to wake him up for something. We cabbed back up to the van, which had now been parked in front of the Ameritania for three hours. These days if you idled a van in Times Square for that long, Homeland Security would be on your ass. Ryan climbed into the front seat and almost immediately fell asleep.

We got to the Saratoga Performing Arts Center three hours late. As soon as we unloaded, Ryan set aside his black Les Paul and his amp—the ultraloud Fender Twin Reverb that had emptied the bar in

Aspen. He rolled the amp down a hallway and into a vacant room. Then he locked the door, plugged in the Les Paul, and started blasting away. I was sitting in my little production office, which was near our dressing room. I don't think I've ever heard anything as loud as the sound of Ryan's guitar searing through the SPAC hallway. He was shredding like Hendrix at the Monterey Pop Festival, and it sounded like my head was inside the speaker cone. He was giving *me* an inner-ear disorder. No way Springo was going to let this slide. Sure enough, seconds later he stormed into my production office. "Goddammit!" he yelled. "Get fucking Hammerhead to turn off that fucking guitar! Right now!"

I walked down the hallway, the Les Paul getting louder with every step. I banged on the door for a few minutes, and finally Ryan unplugged, a devilish smile on his face.

Whiskeytown had signed on to do only the first half of the Fogerty tour, and that half would be over in a week. So that night, when Fogerty's younger brother Bob (who acted as John's personal manager) pulled me aside, I figured he was going to tell me that our services were no longer needed. Surely Springo had gone to him to complain about Hammerhead and the Les Paul. Or maybe he'd gotten wind of Ryan's onstage antics. I was ready with an apology.

But no. Bob Fogerty pulled me aside to ask if Whiskeytown could stick around for the second half of the tour. I was stunned. *I* would have shit-canned us.

Because I was now the band's manager, it was my call. And I did shit-can us. I knew that doing another leg would be pointless. Fogerty was getting us nowhere. We weren't moving any merch. We weren't selling any CDs. The crowd didn't care about Ryan, and Ryan was miserable. So when Bob asked, I said thanks but no. I didn't even run the idea by the band.

Waiting to Derail

One month later, in August of 1998, Ryan would do a show in New York at the Mercury Lounge. He didn't check with me first; he just booked the gig. And he didn't play acoustic; he played with a full band. But the show wasn't billed as Whiskeytown. It was billed as Ryan Adams. Solo. Period. He was joined onstage by Mike Daly on guitar, Steven Terry on drums, and Keith Christopher, who was the original bass player for the Georgia Satellites. The Ryan Adams solo gig was a one-off, but it was hard to see it as anything but what it was: a precursor of things to come.

CHAPTER

15

Ryan spent that summer of 1998 largely in New York, working on songs, living the life of an up-and-comer in the big city. He would have loved to just stay in writing/record-making mode, to transition from Christopher Street to the recording studio without bothering with live shows, save for the solo gig he'd done at the Mercury Lounge. Trouble was, in September we had three weeks of West Coast headlining dates on the board. These shows had all been approved by Jacknife before Chris and Jenni got the boot, so like it or not, Ryan was contractually obligated to go back on the road one more time in support of *Strangers Almanac*.

I rented the van and trailer, and we all met up in Boulder, Colorado, for two days of rehearsal before the first show at the Fox Theatre. Ryan and Mike Daly flew in from New York. Caitlin, Brad, and Danny jetted in from Raleigh. Because Jon Wurster had a previous commitment with Superchunk, Steven Terry was back on drums. The revolving door that had spun him out of Whiskeytown had whisked around and put him back behind the kit.

Waiting to Derail

Ryan was in a crabby mood right out of the gate. Maybe it was because he'd played the Mercury Lounge show and was now thinking ahead to a time when Whiskeytown didn't exist, when all the marquees would read *Tonight: Ryan Adams*. Then again, he'd been thinking post-Whiskeytown pretty much since the band's formation. At any rate, he was pissed about having to leave New York. He focused his anger on the conditions of the rehearsal place I'd booked: a spare room in the warehouse of a drum manufacturing company, way on the outskirts of town. When it came to practice spots, there just wasn't much choice in Boulder, especially for a band whose album had been out for a year and whose sales were a disappointment. I reserved the one place we could afford.

For whatever reason, Ryan found the spot lacking, and his irritation set the tone for the rest of the tour. The Boulder show was half-baked, but the next gig—at the Zephyr in Salt Lake City—flat-out sucked. Afterward, a girl walked up to Mike Daly and handed him a note that read: *My friends and I drove five hours to see you. Strangers Almanac is our favorite album ever. I can't believe we came all this way here for such a crappy show.*

Whenever Ryan caught word of negative fan feedback like this, he obviously didn't respond by gathering the band around in a circle and saying, "You know what, guys? That show was a little bit unfair to the crowd. We can do better. We can try harder." Instead, using my laptop, he'd go on the Internet and type out a drunken minimanifesto, something to the extent of: *Rock and roll isn't safe and tame. It's an uncaged tiger, and if you get too close, you're gonna get bit.*

On the long drive from Salt Lake to Portland, we stopped at a travel plaza where Ryan bought a pair of goofy-looking glasses. They were like the Groucho Marx-style novelty item, but instead of the big nose and fuzzy mustache, they came with a monkey nose. I took this as a positive sign. Wacky Ryan was much more fun to be around than angry Ryan.

The Portland show was at the Crystal Ballroom, a turn-of-the-century dance hall with a floor that bounced so that couples could tango and fox-trot all night long. The place held fifteen hundred people, but there was also a setup where you could put four hundred in a corner and it looked intimate but not empty.

Earlier in the summer, Ryan and I had talked about who the opening act for the West Coast run should be. Previously, Jacknife had always picked the support act, which was usually one of their other clients. But now that I was manager, I had a say in booking the opener. A buddy of ours in Chapel Hill was working with a power pop act from Richmond by way of Milwaukee called Maki, and Ryan and I both loved the demo our friend had given us. They were poppy and sloppy, in a Replacements kind of way.

"Dude," Ryan said to me. "Let's bring those Maki guys out." He was long past giving a shit about booking an opener for a practical reason, like, say, to boost attendance or to repay a favor. We decided to bring along a band with no record deal that nobody'd ever heard of. Why? Because they were great.

Maki barely had any merch, no CDs to sell. They didn't even have a van. They toured in a rental car, and in our trailer we stashed what little gear they had. We'd arranged for them to get two hundred bucks a show. And at the end of the night, when I'd go to collect their money, promoters would ask me, "Why am I paying two hundred dollars for a support act I've never heard of?"

I'd snag the cash and say, "Because that's who Ryan wants."

The Maki guys drank like soldiers. Every night. Hammered by the time they took the stage. I don't know if Whiskeytown was influencing them or vice versa, but there was definitely an alcohol arms race happening between the two bands—mutual assured intoxication.

After the Portland show, we piled into the van to head back to the hotel, a Howard Johnson's out by the airport. It was about 2:00 a.m., and the van was loaded with drunken, postshow musicians. The six Whiskeytowners. Two or three Maki dudes. Plus our new soundguy, Big Travis, and our new roadie, Robbie, who we all called Suave Robbé. (Ryan had had enough of my buddy Ace—who was a hard worker but also a fun-loving goofball who could be exhausting to hang around with, especially if you hadn't been friends with him for twenty years, as I had.) Everyone was yelling and screaming. The stereo was cranked. It was chaos. Ryan sat in the passenger seat. Behind the wheel, I zigzagged the van and trailer out of downtown.

Soon I was driving down Sandy Boulevard, a long four-lane road full of car dealerships, warehouses, and shuttered stores. When I was idled at a stoplight, I looked out the passenger window and saw that a lowered Honda Accord had pulled up next to us. I also owned an Accord; it was parked in my driveway back in Durham. But while mine was an old hatchback, this car sitting beside us in Portland was all tricked out with neon underbody lights and a douchey-looking spoiler. The light turned green, and I hit the gas. So did the other guy.

We stopped at the next light, and the Accord pulled up beside us. Now I could see that inside the car were two white kids in their midtwenties. Rap wannabe dudes. So far, there'd been no confrontation. We'd looked at them, they at us. That's it. The light changed and we both accelerated. Everybody was still hooting and hollering, the stereo still blasting. Ryan reached into the center console and grabbed the monkey glasses.

We pulled up to the third stoplight, and again the underlit, spoilered-up Accord pulled alongside us. But now Ryan was wearing those monkey glasses. He looked at the kids in the Accord. They looked at him. Ha-ha-ha. It was all in good fun. It was now about 2:30, and we were the only two cars on the road. Then I saw Ryan's window go down. It was September, warm in the Pacific Northwest, a beautiful night.

Ryan leaned out his window. The driver in the Accord rolled his window down. Then from behind the monkey glasses, Ryan said, "I think your spoiler sucks."

"Fuck you!" the driver yelled.

The light turned green and we took off. Now those guys were driving like they wanted to strangle us. They cut in front of me, behind me, beside me—swerving like stunt drivers. They pulled up and gave us the finger, which set all the drunks in my van howling. "Fuck you! Fuck you!"

This went on for ten minutes, but it seemed like two hours. We were still the only two vehicles on the road. The Accord cut in front of me, and I slowed down. Then they slowed down. So I sped up. Then they sped up, everybody yelling, middle fingers getting a workout. I tried to think of some way to lose them, but in a fifteen-passenger van with a loaded six-foot-by-twelve-foot trailer off the back, we weren't exactly maneuverable. I looked for a convenience store with a cop sitting in the lot. Nothing. I could not shake those guys. And the whole time there was a swirl of screaming: "Fuck you, fuck you, fuck you!"

We were getting close to the Howard Johnson's, but driving to the hotel was the last thing I was going to do. Even if I got safely parked, those dickheads would know where we were staying.

They could come back and smash the windows or slash the tires. They were still on my tail. I had to think of something.

So I slowed way down, and they sailed right past. Now they were about 150 yards ahead of me. In front of them, the light turned red. The Accord stopped. The length of a football field behind him, I stopped. Smack in the middle of Sandy Boulevard. For a few seconds both vehicles idled there.

Then the Accord driver opened the door, and he got out of the car. He started walking toward the van, erect, determined, like he was packing a gun. From a hundred yards back, I was squinting, wondering what my move was. And over the din of all the *fuck you*s, I could hear Steven Terry in the very back of the van yelling, "Thomas, just run him over! Kill him!" He kept repeating it: Run him over! Kill him! I clicked on the highbeams. The dude stopped. He was still as a statue in the middle of the road. My heart was pounding.

I stomped on the accelerator. Now that he was out of the car, my plan was to race past him. I was gunning it, going as fast as I could make the van move, still listening to this swirl of drunken screaming, and slowly the yelling morphed from *Fuck you!* and *Run him over!* to *Stop! Stop! Stop!* I was almost even with the Accord, within maybe thirty feet of the guy standing in the road. I was looking straight ahead, because I didn't want to accidentally run the dude over. Suddenly, the message from behind me came through clear as a bell: "Stopppppppp!"

I hit brakes as hard as I could. The van lurched to a stop, my chest pushed toward the steering wheel. I looked to my right, past Ryan and out the passenger window. There was the rap wannabe dude, standing in the road by his car. And there was Steven Terry, the drummer, standing right next to the Accord, disheveled, with his pants all ripped and scuffed, ready to scrap West Virginia-style. I was totally confused. Steven Terry outside the van did not compute. *What the fuck?*

Twenty seconds earlier, before I'd stomped on the gas, Steven had been sitting back in the last row, yelling, "Kill him! Run him over!" Tired of talk and ready for action, he popped open the rear doors, scooted his ass up onto the headrests, and was about to climb out the back. That's when I floored it. The force of the acceleration threw him out the doors. He dropped maybe five feet, but instead of hitting the pavement, he landed on the hitch, in the space between the van and the trailer. While I was racing to get the fuck out of there, he was holding onto the bar of the trailer hitch, his legs dragging on the pavement that was sliding under him at twenty, thirty, forty miles per hour. When I slammed on the brakes, he let go of the bar, hit the ground, and, like a Hollywood stuntman, rolled out of the path of the trailer before it could slam into him.

Seconds later, I saw him out the window, jeans torn and frayed, ready to whip some tricked-out-Accord-driving ass. The rap wannabee dude looked at him, let out a mocking Bart Simpson laugh, "Ha-ha," and climbed into his car. The Accord roared out of there. As Steven climbed into the side doors of the van, all he said was, "Gawd damn, dude."

I slid the van into gear and tried my best to drive us to the hotel. My arms were shaking. My legs were shaking. Steven Terry could have died. He should have died. Anybody else would have died. They would have hit the ground between the van and the trailer. And just like that the trailer—which weighed nearly two thousand pounds empty—would have bashed their head and run them over.

Steven Terry spent the night at the Howard Johnson's instead of at the Multnomah County Morgue thanks to one thing and one thing only: his world-class redneck athleticism.

Waiting to Derail

The next night was Vancouver. Good crowd, fine show. All was going well until Suave Robbé—the guitar tech who had replaced Ace—accidentally put the strap of Ryan's '64 Gibson Firebird on backwards. During a mid-set guitar change, when Ryan was pulling the guitar over his head to swap it for another instrument, the backwards strap jabbed Ryan in the mouth. Ryan was extremely *displeased*. As the look on his face darkened, I braced myself. I didn't know what Ryan was about to do, but I knew it was going to be bad.

Ryan had only owned the Firebird for four months. I remember how excited he was the day he got it. It was back in May, a couple of weeks before the start of the Fogerty Tour. I was in Durham making preparations, and Ryan was out in Los Angeles doing some recording with Tommy Stinson, bass player from the Replacements. One day Ryan called me from California. "Aw, man!" he said. "Guess what?" Just from the tone of his voice, I could tell how fired up he was. It was like Santa had promised him a ride on the sleigh. "I just got two free guitars!"

He told me that the first guitar was a midseventies Gibson L-5S Custom, a mint-condition solid body similar to the one Keith Richards borrowed from Ronnie Wood and then took on tour with the X-Pensive Winos. The second free guitar was the '64 Firebird, which I'd later find out was in such perfect shape, it was like it had spent the last thirty-four years sealed in a vacuum tube.

"This is awesome!" he said. "Two guitars. Worth seven thousand dollars. They were free!"

First rule about rare guitars: they don't come free. "How on earth did you get them?" I asked Ryan. "Who bought them for you?"

"The guy from Bug Music. He said I had some money in my account, so he went ahead and paid for 'em. Two free guitars! Seven thousand dollars. *Seven thousand* dollars!"

Bug Music was the company that administered the publishing rights and royalties for Ryan's songs. That month, a movie called *Hope Floats* had been released, starring Sandra Bullock and Harry Connick Jr. The soundtrack featured a Whiskeytown tune called "Wither, I'm a Flower." Fortunately for Ryan and every other artist with a song in the film, the soundtrack also included Garth Brooks's "To Make You Feel My Love," which became a number-one country single. Thanks to mighty Garth, the soundtrack would go double platinum, peaking at number one on the *Billboard* Country album chart and at number four on the *Billboard* Top 200. Four of us from the Whiskeytown camp would eventually get platinum records to hang on our wall. Ryan, Caitlin, and I got the first three. The fourth went to Ryan's cat. It probably hung right over the litter box.

That day on the phone, it struck me again that for all his talent, Ryan was still just twenty-three. There were a lot of lessons he'd yet to learn. "Ryan," I said, "Listen. Those guitars weren't free. The Bug Music guy paid for them with *your* publishing money. *You* bought those guitars."

After a few seconds, it dawned on him that I was right. "Ugh," he said. I thought I heard his palm smack his forehead. "Seven thousand dollars." Then he laughed. Ryan didn't care about money, and he didn't waste time beating himself up about mistakes.

Now, on stage in Vancouver after getting jabbed by the strap, Ryan took off the Firebird and held it upside down. With his fingers curled over the body, he pointed the neck down toward the stage. Then, like road worker wielding a jackhammer, he drove the Firebird into the ground, headstock first. The neck snapped. The guitar was destroyed.

The punk rock dude in me loved to see Ryan get pissed off and smash shit, but this had crossed the line from punk to something else, something sad and desperate. The guitar collector in me wanted to throw up. This was not fun or funny. It was disgusting. If Ryan hadn't splintered it, that guitar today would be worth twelve or fifteen thousand dollars. Maybe more. Of course, the moment Ryan did splinter it, every other '64 Firebird in the world increased slightly in value because now there was one less of them.

Maybe the saddest thing was that Ryan *loved* that guitar. It was the other "free" guitar, the Gibson L-5S, that he hated. He'd later tell me that he wanted to smash that guitar, too. I told him that if he ever busted up the L-5S, I would fucking kill him.

After the Vancouver show, I placed the Firebird back into its case, piece by piece. Like a broken body into a coffin.

It's stomach-turning to watch a dude destroy the thing he loves.

CHAPTER

16

W e crossed back into the United States and played Seattle's Bumbershoot festival the next day. It was a big, outdoor show, and it should have been fun. But I was still feeling pissed off and dejected. While Whiskeytown was playing, I didn't even pretend to work. I plopped down in the grass and watched the show like a regular-old ticket holder. Ryan had started this run all whiny and bitchy in Boulder, and the tour had only gone downhill since. The shows had mostly sucked. I'd nearly killed the drummer. Everything about Whiskeytown now seemed dark and depressing. Right there in the grass, I decided that I couldn't take it anymore. I couldn't put up with *him* anymore. That night in the hotel I wrote a letter to Ryan, telling him I was quitting.

But I never gave it to him. The next morning, after a good night's sleep, I ripped it up. I couldn't quit. I wasn't just the tour manager anymore. For the time being, anyway, I was the artist manager. Sure, Ryan was a pain in the ass, but he was also a supreme talent. For the opportunity of working with a one-in-a-million songwriter like that, I could put up with a little frustration. Plus I'd promised him back at the Waffle House outside Nashville that I would stick with him as long as he would stick with me. Besides, if I had quit—if I'd woken up that morning and flown from Seattle back to Raleigh tail-between-legs—I would have missed everything that happened the next night at the Fillmore in San Francisco.

A lot of people remember the Fillmore show, and naturally everyone thinks their version of what went down that night is the one true story. But there isn't just one true story. Nobody's memory is 100 percent objectively factual—including mine, of course. That said, my memory is pretty damn solid. Plus I was sober.

Here's what happened.

The Fillmore is sacred ground. Rock-and-roll church. On par in music history with Harlem's Apollo Theater and Nashville's Ryman Auditorium. Starting in the midsixties, the legendary promoter Bill Graham booked pretty much everybody into the Fillmore: The Who, the Dead, the Doors. Hendrix, Creedence, Zeppelin. And on and on. Along the way, Graham defined what it meant to be a rock promoter. He invented backstage catering. He helped make concert posters into an art form, and whenever the show sold out, everyone in attendance got copies of that night's poster. Near the front door there was a big tub of free apples. Everybody who worked there was friendly and kind—old hippies who greeted you with "Welcome to the Fillmore." During our load-in and sound check, if I'd knocked back a shot of bourbon every time somebody from the staff asked me "Is there anything else I can do for you?" I would have been plastered by showtime.

Whiskeytown had never played the Fillmore, and my hope was that—as with Radio City Music Hall—the prominence and history of the venue would demand Ryan's interest. I watched the show from the side of the stage. All was going fine. Better than fine, actually. The band was tight, and the crowd of about 250—not bad for a Tuesday—was digging it. As the set approached the end, I gave myself an imaginary pat on the back for having the smarts not to give Ryan my resignation letter.

Then the band launched into the last tune of the night, "Piss on Your Fucking Grave," a full-blast punk rock song that has exactly zero to do with alt-country. The chorus: *Fuck you, fuck you, fuck off.* Down in hell, GG Allin—who died of a heroin overdose in 1993— nodded along appreciatively. On stage, Ryan was jumping around, flailing about. He was selling the song's message, fully committed. It was refreshing to see him so into what he was singing.

In the crowd, though, the alt-country devotees radiated confusion, steadily moving toward belligerence. They'd discovered they'd been hoodwinked. *Wait a second. This isn't country music. Where's the lapsteel? Why's this song about a hundred beats per minute too fast?* The energy in the room turned. Nobody yelled *Judas!*—as an audience member had twenty-two years earlier in Manchester, England, when Bob Dylan unexpectedly went electric on them—but it seemed like lots of them were thinking it. Then somebody threw a cup at Ryan.

He kept rocking. Singing sweetly but with venom. *Fuck you, fuck you, fuck off.* In those words, I heard: *Fuck you, Bill Graham. Fuck you, Fillmore. Fuck off, rock-and-roll sacred ground. I'll take a hot, steaming piss on the lot of it.* And as he sang, the "you" seemed to expand: *Fuck you, sports bars and ski towns. Fuck you, music critics and disc jockeys. Fuck off, Fogerty fans and Firebird guitars.* He was pissing on the grave of *No Depression* magazine. Pissing on the grave of Outpost Records. Pissing on the grave of the whole damn music business. Saying *fuck you* to the idea that Ryan Adams was alt-country's Kurt Cobain. Fuck you to everybody who had expectations for who and what Ryan Adams was supposed to be. And fuck off to the Ryan Adams he'd created for himself.

The song crescendoed to a big, AC/DC-style finish, and during that wash of power chords and crash cymbals, Ryan kicked one of the monitor wedges off the front of the stage. It fell about five feet and slammed to the floor of the Fillmore. An audible *boo* from the crowd. More detritus flew from the audience to the stage. Later Ryan would claim that he had problems with the monitors, that he was unable to hear himself sing. In his defense, we didn't have a monitor engineer with us, so we were at the mercy of whatever stage sound the house gave us. Still: Ryan had played the whole set without complaining about the sound, so the monitors weren't the issue. The issue was that Ryan wanted to put one final *fuck you!* into a song that was already full of them. The monitor dropped like the exclamation point.

One wedge down, Ryan looked over at a second wedge. I knew he was thinking about double exclamation points. But before his foot hit the speaker, the house monitor engineer jumped out from behind his desk and grabbed Ryan. Mike Daly then grabbed the monitor guy. There was pushing and elbowing, as more Fillmore staff members took the stage. In the chaos, Ryan somehow slipped to the dressing room, which was just off stage right. Steven Terry and I followed him in. I locked the door.

"That was awesome," Steven said, breathing like a vandal who'd just outrun the cops. Somebody pounded on the door.

Ryan laughed. "Fuck this place."

He had fucked with the Fillmore. He'd pissed not just on the grave but inside the church. And that was precisely his point.

Fuck Bill Graham. Fuck Bill Graham's club. Whiskeytown doesn't discriminate. There are no sacred cows. We put on our same show no matter where we're playing.

But now, those same hippies who a few hours earlier were asking if there's was anything else they could do for us were ready to beat our asses. Peace and love was yesterday's news. The guys banging on the door wanted to rip out Ryan's trachea.

"Listen," I said to Ryan and Steven. "We need to get you out of here. Right now. These stagehands want to kill you."

"Fuck them," Steven said.

"This is serious." I said, leaning against the door, a one-man barricade. "You've got to listen to me right now." I heard an increasing commotion from the other side of the door, a chorus of hippies shouting, "Fuck you!" But the pounding had stopped. Maybe somebody was heading to the production office to get the key to the door. "Okay, guys," I said to my two band members. "Here's what's going to happen."

I told them that I was going to open the door, and the second I did, the three of us were going to take off running. As fast as we could. Me in the front. Ryan in the middle. Steven in back. "You guys follow me, and I'll get you out of here," I said. "Are you ready?"

They said they were.

"I'm going to be *running*," I said. "Are you *ready?*"

They nodded.

"Okay," I said. "Let's go."

I opened the door, and we bolted down to the floor. The crowd of about 250 had already cleared out, so the floor was wide open except for the mess of cups and cans. I aimed catty-corner for the rear of the building, where I knew there was a door that opened to an outside staircase. The three of us were about halfway to the exit when I heard somebody yell, "Hey, there he is!" A stagehand pointed at Ryan and then started chasing us. A few others joined him.

The door opened to a landing that was about three stories above street level. From there, the staircase ran down the side of the building. I let Ryan and Steven through. At the top of the stairs, I looked out across Geary Boulevard, and I saw a building with neon signs in the windows. "Go to that bar across the street," I told them. "I'll come get you later."

As Ryan and Steven descended the staircase, the stagehands appeared at the landing. I stretched my arms from handrail to handrail so they couldn't get past.

"Hey, man!" one of the staff members yelled toward Ryan, who was about halfway down. "That was bullshit, what you just did!"

Ryan turned around, flipped the bird, and yelled, "Fuck you!"

While Ryan and Steven waited at the bar across Geary, I had to go try to collect our guarantee. Time to man up and face the music. The manager was surprisingly calm about the whole thing, much calmer than his hippie enforcers had been. But his calmness didn't mean we were getting paid.

"I'm keeping your fifteen hundred until we find out how much it's gonna cost to get that wedge fixed," he told me. If there was anything left after fixing the monitor, he'd mail a check to our booking agent. This was a reasonable solution, but we were on a lean budget. Not getting the cash that night hurt.

After load-out, I walked across the street to collect Ryan and Steven. First I asked Ryan to come outside. Alone. I pulled two cigarettes out of a pack and gave him one. We sat down on the sidewalk across from the Fillmore and smoked.

"Tomorrow in Los Angeles I'm going to buy you two guns," I said.

He took a drag. "Why's that?"

"So you can shoot yourself in both feet at the same time."

Neither of us laughed. We just sat there smoking on the sidewalk. I looked at Ryan. I looked at the Fillmore. I felt worn out and beaten up. At the last gig, I'd written the "I quit" letter. The show before that was Vancouver and the smashed Firebird. The night before that I'd almost decapitated Steven Terry. And that was just the last four shows. I had been putting up with this for over a year. It was just too much. I felt like I was about to cry.

"Ryan," I said, "is there ever going to be a day when you just show up and play a normal show? When you act like a normal person and not do all this shit?" I turned and looked right at him. "Is that day ever going to happen?"

"I don't know, man," he said. Tilting his head back, he blew a slow stream of smoke. "Maybe. Someday."

We headed to Los Angeles for two shows at the Whiskey a Go Go. Months back, when these gigs were originally scheduled, the band's booking agent, Scott Clayton, asked if he could add an additional support act to the bill. Opening at the Whiskey was a gem of a slot, too good to just give to an unknown band like Maki. The Maki guys would still open both nights, but Scott added another act to each show. The first night, it was a new band from San Francisco called Train. When I met them at load-in, I learned that they were huge fans of Ryan and Whiskeytown, and they were super-fired up to be added to the bill. I didn't know it yet, but just over a year later, I'd be working as *their* tour manager.

The 1998 MTV Video Awards were taped in Los Angeles on the same night as the first Whiskey show, so lots of musicians and celebrities were out and about on the Sunset Strip. Wynona Ryder—who'd already established a reputation for dating musicians—was allegedly in the crowd at the Whiskey, and Ryan kept running around backstage saying, "Winona's after me. She's after me." Ryan and Winona would eventually become friends, and they may or may not have dated (Ryan has been cagey about confirming this). But I'm not sure they even spoke that night at the Whiskey. I think he was just excited that she'd shown up. When famous actresses start coming to your gigs, it's hard not to be excited.

During the set that first night, Green Day's Billie Joe Armstrong walked up to the stage and tried to hand Ryan a cocktail. But Ryan wouldn't take it from him. After the show was over, I said, "Why didn't you take that drink from Billie Joe?"

"Man," he said, "you always told me not to take drinks from strangers."

"That's true," I said. "But a famous rock star isn't the same as a stranger." It was so cool, though, how in offering the drink, Billie Joe hadn't seemed like a rock star at all. He was just a dude in the audience, recognizing that the dude onstage might be thirsty. "Don't worry, Ryan," I said. "Billie Joe's not going to poison you." I smiled and gave him a squeeze on the shoulder. "At least not in front of a sold-out crowd."

After the second show, the band spent a few days recording in Los Angeles. Then we'd make the thirteen-hundred-mile drive to Austin for the final three shows of this run. Ryan was not looking forward to a twenty-four-hour van ride. For the last week, we'd been staying at Sunset and La Brea, and at the topless bar across the street from the hotel, Ryan had apparently run into David Lee Roth and

Lemmy Kilmister. I knew that Ryan could care less about strippers, but there was no way he was going to ride in a hot van across the Sonoran Desert when the alternative was to belly up at the bar next to Lemmy from Motörhead. He decided that he and Mike Daly were going to stay in Los Angeles for as long as possible and then catch a flight to Austin.

Every time I'd agreed to let Ryan arrive by plane on show day, something bad had happened. So obviously, I didn't want to let them do it. And Ryan knew I didn't want to let them do it. He knew he needed bargaining power. He'd smashed the '64 Firebird, but he still had the other "free guitar," the Gibson L-5S Custom, which he didn't like.

"I'll make you a deal," he said to me. "If you buy us two plane tickets to Austin, I'll give you that guitar."

So Ryan and Mike Daly stayed in Los Angeles for two extra days, while the rest of us drove straight to Austin in one long shot. I was now the proud owner of the L-5S. Ryan's seven-thousand-dollar investment in vintage guitars had yielded him a grand total of two $250 tickets on Southwest Airlines.

The Austin show was weird because it was Jacknife's home turf, and it was our first gig there since Ryan had fired Chris and Jenni. Ryan seemed a little nervous, but he was on point that night— maybe because of those jitters.

Dallas was also strong, and Ryan was noticeably sober. Early in the night, he and I watched the Maki set from the crowd. As usual, the openers were wasted. Up onstage the singer had taken his shirt off, and he was sloppy beyond hilarity, approaching pitifulness.

I leaned over to Ryan and said, "You see that? That was you not long ago."

"No way, man," he said. "You're crazy."

"Nope," I said. "That was you."

The *Fort Worth Star-Telegram* later confirmed my impressions: "Whiskeytown played a remarkable show, especially compared to their last gig at Trees, a few months back, when Adams appeared to be inebriated beyond belief and the band was embarrassingly sloppy. On Friday, a far different image was painted: Adams was in prime form, singing his songs about loneliness and losing with both fire and finesse, and playing guitar with ragged fury."

During the Dallas set, one of Ryan's acoustic guitars fell over and broke, so he smashed it, putting it out if its misery. Back in Vancouver, when he was smashing the Firebird, I read anger and hatred on his face. That act of destruction had been pathetic rather than punk rock. But the guitar sacrifice in Dallas felt lighthearted and mischievous; it was less sadistic and more in the spirit of "Oops. Oh, well." I nodded along approvingly.

That "fuck-it-all" spirit continued the next night in Houston, the last show of this stretch. We were already two guitars down compared to the start the tour. At the end of the Houston show, he destroyed another acoustic. Three guitars down.

Then he walked back toward Steven Terry and started taking apart the drum set. He sent cymbal stands cockeyed. Kicked over the floor tom. "This is the last show of the tour," he said into the mic. "Fuck it!" Then he walked off stage.

"Ryan," I said when I caught up with him. "We're playing The Brewery in like a week." Houston was the last show of this run, but he forgot that we were doing Raleigh in ten days, a gig that would give us the cash we needed to play the last date Whiskeytown had on the board: a radio one-off at Chicago's Navy Pier.

The next day, Ryan flew back to New York. I drove the van back to Raleigh. The trailer was mostly empty, and the little bit of equipment that did remain was hardly in working condition. Back in the spring of 1997, Roldan told me that my job was to tour-manage the launch. Now I was tour-managing the wreckage.

It didn't occurr to me on that long drive home (but maybe it should have) that by the time we'd hit Texas, Ryan had started the process of emptying himself of Whiskeytown—down to the gear. He was already making his not-so-clean break.

CHAPTER

17

I arrived back in North Carolina with a trailer half-full of busted equipment. Counting the blank squares on my calendar, I saw that I had ten days to cobble together enough gear to do two shows: a gig at the Brewery followed by a radio-sponsored Oktoberfest event at Chicago's Navy Pier Ballroom. These were the absolute last dates. The end of the *Strangers Almanac* tour. After Chicago, I would celebrate my own survival by spending a week in Jamaica with Stephanie.

What would come next? I was theoretically managing the band, so my job was to help answer that question. Then again, I wasn't sure how long I'd be able to hold onto the position. Tour managers don't often get promoted to artist management, especially at the big-league level. From the record company's perspective, I didn't have the experience. Still, while the job was mine, I would try to be as legit as possible.

Two months earlier, in the span between the Fogerty tour and the West Coast dates, I reached out to Will Marley, the singer of

Lustre, the first band I'd tour-managed. Will and I decided to start an artist management company together. Empire Entertainment Group. Headquartered in a spare room in my house. Our first move? Add to the roster. We took on a band that had opened for Whiskeytown a few times: Danielle Howle and the Tantrums, from Columbia, South Carolina.

Empire Entertainment now had a name, an office, and two clients—for the time being. All through the West Coast dates, while Ryan was wearing monkey-nose glasses and destroying guitars, whenever I filled out paperwork listing the band's management contact, on the line next to my name, I always wrote "*current* management." In Whiskeytown, *current* was as good as it got, because nobody but Ryan was really *in* Whiskeytown. He was the only one with job security. Caitlin was a necessary component, of course, but she still wasn't in the band from a legal standpoint. Mike Daly had played nearly every show on the *Strangers Almanac* tour, but he wasn't officially in the band, either. He was still trying to make himself invaluable to Ryan. We all knew that Whiskeytown was whatever Ryan wanted it to be. If he wanted it to develop into a thirty-year experiment, he could. If he wanted it to peter out and fade away, then that's what would happen.

Now, as I got ready for the final two gigs of the tour, a new complication: the Navy Pier show was a Whiskeytown *flydate*, meaning that we'd travel by plane, bringing only guitars with us. We'd rent the rest of the gear (the "backline," as it's called) in Chicago. Putting *Whiskeytown* and *flydate* in the same sentence is a frightening proposition. The band had never done a show like this before. It was hard enough to get everybody loaded into an Econoline, let alone a Boeing. So far, my batting average when trying to deliver Ryan to a gig via airplane was piss-poor.

Being an inexperienced dumb-ass of a manager, I thought it would be smart to do a Brewery show the night before Navy Pier. Make a little cash in Raleigh to offset the costs of Chicago. This was my blue-collar, punk rock ethos working overtime. The Brewery show was no problem. The challenge was waking everybody up the next morning and getting them to the airport.

The crew and I took an early flight so we could arrive at Navy Pier in time to get the stage set up. The band was supposed to fly in later. You don't have to be Nostradamus to predict what happened. Ryan overslept. Missed his flight. I called Becker, the travel agent, and had Ryan rebooked, but when he got the airport, he refused to board the aircraft. He wanted to switch carriers. From an airport pay phone, Ryan called Becker. "I want to fly on American Airlines," he said. "I like the color of their planes better." So Becker rebooked him again. Sure sign you're a rock star: one man, three plane tickets.

The last show of the *Strangers Almanac* tour was an encapsulation of the eighteen months that had led up to it. Ryan drank too much. The set was too short. It started with complaints about how the crowd wasn't paying attention and ended with kicked-over mic stands. Man, I needed a week on the beach in Jamaica.

But missing planes is apparently contagious. I was so exhausted after the show that I overslept and didn't make my flight.

Everybody else left Chicago the day after the Navy Pier gig, but Ryan stayed in the Windy City for a few extra days to work on some tunes with James Iha from Smashing Pumpkins. All through that fall of 1998, Ryan was in full-blast songwriting mode, primarily composing on piano. He was constantly sending new tunes to Outpost, constantly thinking about the next record.

[205]

Waiting to Derail

In mid-December James Iha flew to Raleigh. I drove to the airport in my crappy Accord hatchback and picked him up. We'd decided to do a last-minute, largely unannounced show at the Local 506 in Chapel Hill, where James would join Whiskeytown on stage. But instead of calling it Whiskeytown, we billed the band as the Kids. I drew up a flyer, made copies at Kinko's, and stapled them to the Franklin Street kiosks. *The Kids. Local 506. Tonight. 5 Bucks.*

The band did four days of rehearsal, and when not practicing, Ryan and James either hung out at my house in the Durham suburbs or drank in Raleigh or Chapel Hill. Meanwhile, we spread details of the show via word of mouth and on Internet message boards, so at the Local 506 that night, there was a nice crowd. But the show was low energy. Sloppy and sleepy. Even though the set included a bunch of new songs, it was obvious that Whiskeytown had run its course. Everybody was burned out. Other than cement Ryan and James's friendship, The Kids gig didn't accomplish much. Mostly it put the band's lack of enthusiasm on public display.

Soon it was January of 1999, and there wasn't a single Whiskeytown date on the calendar. Ryan spent most of his time in New York, where he and Amy moved to a different apartment. Their new place was in the East Village, on Avenue A, just down the street from a rock club called Brownies and just up the street from Niagara, a bar that D Gen's Jesse Malin coowned. This is the neighborhood where Ryan really wanted to be. Christopher Street had been cool and all, in a West Village-folk kind of way. But the East Village was cooler. Grittier. It was one of the strands in punk rock's DNA. The East Village meant Johnny Thunders and Dee Dee Ramone. Allen Ginsberg and Jim Carroll. St. Marks and Tompkins Square Park.

Ryan and I would talk on the phone once or twice a week, often late at night after he and Amy had had a fight. He'd tell me he wanted to come home to North Carolina. I'd tell him to hop on the Amtrak and head south, or I'd offer to buy him a plane ticket. But in the morning they'd kiss and make up, and he'd decide to stick it out on Avenue A. I wouldn't hear from him for a few days.

Meanwhile, Ryan's attorney had suggested that I look for a partner to comanage Whiskeytown with Will and me, somebody with more experience. "You're good at keeping Ryan on track most of the time," he said. "But Outpost is not going to let you do this by yourself."

So as Ryan got ready to record the next album, Will and I made trips to New York and elsewhere, meeting with established managers to see if we could find the perfect fit—for Ryan and for the record company. We spoke to lots of people, including Ken Levitan, who would later found the behemoth, Nashville-based Vector Management, and whose roster would include Emmylou Harris, Lyle Lovett, Kings of Leon, Cheap Trick, and many more. But we hadn't yet found the right piece to the puzzle.

Because Ryan wasn't doing any gigs, I wasn't making any money. Even the best manager in the world can't outwit math: 15 percent of nothing is nothing. Making matters more urgent, I now had a wedding to plan (and pay for). In January, on my thirty-fifth birthday, I had proposed to Stephanie, and we set the date for October. I needed to work. So I took a job tour-managing D Generation on a run of dates opening for the Offspring, who were doing arenas in support of their *Americana* album, the one with the single "Pretty Fly for a White Guy."

The Offspring guys were so generous, the most considerate people you could ever meet. Every night after sound check, the drummer, Ron Welty, took his kit down off the riser so that the opening bands—D Gen and the Living End—could set their kits up there, which gave everybody more room to move on stage. Even in small clubs it was hard to find headliners willing to strike their drums for the opening acts; on an arena tour, this small kindness was unheard of. Apparently, back when the Offspring were opening for bigger bands, Welty got so frustrated trying to squeeze his kit in front of the headliner's kit, he promised himself that if he ever became the headliner, he'd strike his drums.

It was encouraging to meet such nice people, and—compared to Whiskeytown—the job was simple. I never once had to talk Jesse Malin into taking the stage. The shows were fun but also a little heartbreaking, because D Generation was grinding to a halt. The band was touring behind their third album, *Through the Darkness*, which was getting no support from the label. The record was dead on arrival. It's a blast to be on tour when everything's going well: your song is on the radio, you're selling records. Everyone's high-fiving and hugging and getting checks in the mail. But when you can feel your career going down the tubes? Being out on the road sucks.

In April, D Generation played a headlining show in New York at Coney Island High, another bar that Jesse Malin had a stake in. It was billed as their final gig ever. Come last call, they were going to break up (they'd eventually reunite for a few shows in 2008 and 2011 before doing some recording with Ryan in 2013 and releasing a new record in 2016). Stephanie and I drove up from Durham for the gig, crashing on an air mattress at Amy and Ryan's apartment on Avenue A. The four of us had a great time at the show, but the reason *for* the show was sad. I ran lights for D Gen that night, and standing at the light board, I thought back to a moment after the very last date on the Offspring tour. We were riding on the bus, leaving the final show in Philadelphia and heading to New York to drop everybody off. "Well," said Danny Sage, D Gen's guitar player, "this is the last time any of us will ride on a bus for a long, long time." It felt like a punch to the gut. Because I knew he was right.

As I worked the faders on the lighting controller at Coney Island High, I couldn't help but think about Whiskeytown. Would Ryan, Caitlin, and I ever again ride on a bus together?

Soon after that, I got a call from Amy, who was still working for Warner Bros. Records. She had a line on a potential gig for me. Warner was looking for somebody to travel that summer with one of their artists, a teenage pop singer. They already had a tour manager on board. Now they needed a utility person to drive the van, run the lights, and lend an experienced hand.

"This might be beneath you a little bit," Amy said, "but if you're interested, I'll pass on your contact information."

"Who's the artist?" I said.

"She's brand new," Amy said. "Her name is Mandy Moore."

I didn't know Mandy Moore from Minnie Mouse, but I followed up on Amy's lead. And once my phone started ringing that spring, it kept ringing. I got two more calls, one right after the other. The first was from a guy named Jay Wilson asking if I was available to tour-manage Train, the band from San Francisco that had been added to the bill at the Whiskey in Los Angeles. The second was a gig tour-managing the Marvelous 3, fronted by Butch Walker. It just so happened that Train and the Marvelous 3 were scheduled to play a radio station show at Raleigh's Walnut Creek Amphitheatre, so I saw both of them live on the same night.

The Marvelous 3 was the perfect rock band. Loud, with killer hooks and big choruses. Music-wise, they were right up my alley. I *loved* them. Train was kind of hippie-dippy back then, and there was definitely some bongo drum action on stage. But their singer, Pat Monahan, was world-class. He was a nice guy, very hardworking and very determined.

Two years earlier, I would have leapt at the chance to do either gig. But now I had to pass on both. By then I'd already committed to doing the Mandy Moore tour. And I was still trying to track down a comanager for Ryan. Plus I was planning a wedding. The Mandy tour would give me enough free time to take care of everything else I was dealing with.

Meanwhile, Whiskeytown started recording at Dreamland Studios in Hurley, New York, just outside of Woodstock. The band, to the extent that there *was* a band, consisted of Ryan, Caitlin, Mike Daly, and a cadre of additional players, including James Iha and Tommy Stinson. Ethan Johns played drums. He also produced the sessions. Given that Ethan was the son of legendary producer Glyn Johns—who had worked with the Rolling Stones, the Who, Dylan, the Clash, and an unparalleled list of giants—his pedigree was attractive to a student of the game like Ryan.

One day when I was in Manhattan to see Danielle Howle— the other act I was managing—I volunteered to drive Ryan and Ethan up to Dreamland. Ethan and his assistant were flying into Newark, and Ryan and I showed up at the baggage claim curb in my beat-up hatchback. Because I was still so naive, I didn't know that I should have hired a car service. Instead, I squeezed Ethan and his assistant into the back seat for the two-hour drive upstate. Sorry, Ethan.

Dreamland was an old converted church, and Ethan had filled it with a jaw-dropping array of cool vintage gear. Thanks to his dad's prominence, he'd grown up in the belly of seventies British rock. This gave him access to instruments and equipment that regular gear-nerds would swoon over, including a Fender Telecaster that was apparently third off the production line. He still owned a guitar that Keith Richards had given to him when he was a kid.

After spending the night upstate, I drove back to Durham. A few days later, I gave Ryan a call up at the studio. I knew that he'd written well over a dozen songs for the album, the working title of which was *Happy Go Bye Bye* but would later be called *Pneumonia*. I also knew that whenever he went into the studio, he got so excited about being there that the song he'd written yesterday would get overshadowed by the new song he wrote today. Being in the studio unleashed a massive flood of creativity that drowned the older material.

"How many songs have you recorded?" I asked him on the phone.

"Eight," he said.

"How many of those are brand new?"

"Eight."

He neglected to tell me something that I'd only learn years later. Apparently, a few nights earlier, he, Ethan, Caitlin, and Mike Daly had driven a rental car through the snow to a bar. On the way back, they intentionally drove the car into a snow bank, just to see what would happen. What happened was that the front end of the car got smashed in. After wobbling back to Dreamland, they made the session bass player, Jennifer Condos, return the car to the rental company. As far as I know, Ryan never got an angry call from Outpost. Nobody ever said, "Hey, Ryan. What the heck happened with that rental car?" Maybe they deducted the charges from the recording budget. Or maybe Outpost just ate the cost, the price of doing business with Ryan.

After hearing the piano-based stuff he'd been tinkering with over the last six months, I wasn't surprised that the new recordings were sounding different from *Strangers Almanac*. Less rootsy, more lush and orchestrated. Less *No Depression*, more *Pet Sounds*. Ryan was not going to be constrained by convention, limited to only singing about bourbon and broken hearts over a bed of fiddle and lapsteel. He'd rather raise two middle fingers to the alt-country purists and their expectations.

As big a step forward as the new songs were, it was unclear when or if a new Whiskeytown record would come out. First of all, Ryan seemed increasingly headed toward a solo career. Second, Outpost Records was bogged down in corporate merger muck. Outpost was a subsidiary of Geffen Records, which was part of Universal Music Group, which was owned by Seagram Company Ltd. A year earlier, Seagram had bought PolyGram, which owned Island and A&M and a whole host of other labels. Once Universal and PolyGram merged under the Seagram cocktail umbrella, nobody knew where that would leave a relatively minor component like Outpost.

Here's what I knew for sure: As he bounced between Dreamland and Avenue A, mergers and acquisitions were the last things on Ryan's mind. He was trying to write a masterpiece.

And I was still trying to find the right comanager to help us navigate these murky corporate waters. One day I drove to Nashville and met with Frank Callari, who managed Lucinda Williams and the Mavericks. Callari's office was slick and impressive, with TVs that were airing CNBC—exactly what I would have been watching had I been at home. We sat down and had a long talk. He was a formidable dude. Large in stature and New York tough down to the Yankees cap he wore. I wasn't a huge sports fan, but as a kid I'd lived in Connecticut, so the Yanks were the team I followed. Now, look: you don't pick a manager based on his baseball cap. But with Callari's track record, the TVs showing CNBC, and his allegiance to the Bronx Bombers, the partnership was off to an encouraging start.

By the time I got home, I was sold on Callari. I called Ryan. "He really seems like the right dude," I said.

Callari flew to New York for a sit-down with Ryan. It all went well. Both guys liked each other. After Callari got back to Nashville, I gave him a call. "Alright. Cool," I said. "Ryan's excited. Now let's hash out the details of this comanagement deal."

A few seconds of silence. "*Comanagement?*" he said. He sounded disgusted. Like I had struck out looking with the bases loaded. "I'm not comanaging Ryan with you."

I was stunned. Flabbergasted. I wondered if maybe I hadn't been clear about the comanagement thing. But, no. I'd been completely straightforward. I suppose it was stupid of me to think some guy I met once in the comforting glow of CNBC would partner with me, but I never suspected I'd get totally cut out of the deal.

I needed Ryan to put his foot down and say to Callari, "If you want me, then Thomas comes along, too." But Ryan didn't put his foot down. Instead, he said to me (without really saying it—I got the message regardless), "I've got a bigger-name manager now. You've done your part."

I was pissed.

Waiting to Derail

So I spent that summer on the road with Mandy Moore, the budding pop star from Orlando. She was fifteen, touring behind her debut single, "Candy." My first show with her was in Virginia Beach, where she was playing a side stage, opening for 'N Sync—featuring Justin Timberlake, of course. There was no band. Mandy sang live over a backing track while four dudes danced around her. Her set was four songs, and it was over in fifteen minutes.

She was a great singer. Polite and polished. Sweet as can be. But at fifteen, she had almost no experience playing live. She didn't know, for instance, how to communicate with the monitor engineer in order to get the stage sounding the way she wanted. So I steered her through the logistical aspects of a live show.

And I helped her do her homework. As I looked over her math and science worksheets, the light bulb would flicker on, and I'd start to remember how to answer the geometry and biology questions. "Do you want me to explain this stuff to you," I'd ask her, "or just do it."

"Just do it," she'd say.

Because she was a minor, one of her parents had to be on the road with us at all times. Three weeks out of the month, her mom would be there. The two of us would hang out, tell stories, drink many beers. And then her dad—who was a pilot for American Airlines—would rotate in for a while. They were both really cool, and the tour was a piece of cake. The easiest I'd ever done. Van and trailer. And because there wasn't any musical gear, the trailer was filled with suitcases and costumes. There was nothing to it.

While all this was happening, Ryan was in and out of the studio, splitting his time between Dreamland, Avenue A, and my house in Durham. Ryan had heard of Mandy, of course, because Amy and I were working with her. And Mandy had heard of Ryan because

I'd been telling her stories about him and Whiskeytown. But as far as I know, the two of them didn't officially meet until much later. None of us could have known that ten years after that summer of 1999, Ryan and Mandy would get married. While Ryan was putting the finishing touches on the new record, I was doing geometry problems for his future wife.

CHAPTER

18

In October, Stephanie and I got married in Blowing Rock, a mountain town in western North Carolina. Ryan was a groomsman in the wedding party, so he flew down with Amy from New York. But they didn't show up at the rehearsal dinner the night before the ceremony. After dinner, some buddies and I did a little barhopping. Downtown Blowing Rock is small, so I figured that if Ryan and Amy were actually in town, there was a good chance we'd run into them.

All summer I'd been out with Mandy, who was now opening for the Backstreet Boys. Ryan and Ethan Johns were finished recording in upstate New York, and the next Whiskeytown album was tentatively scheduled for a release in early 2000. However, because we didn't yet know how the fallout from the Universal/PolyGram merger would affect Outpost, that early 2000 date seemed like wishful thinking. Maybe the Ethan Johns sessions would go the way of the *Forever Valentine* project: fun and urgent while it happened but destined never to get a proper release.

Waiting to Derail

Ryan wasn't going to sit on his hands while the attorneys and executives did their haggling. For him, songwriting is like breathing. His heart can't beat without it. Like always, he was cranking out new tunes, doing demos, playing solo acoustic shows in New York and North Carolina. The Mandy tour had taken me to New York, so I saw him a couple times in the East Village that summer and early fall. He'd become a regular at Punk Rock/Heavy Metal Karaoke night at Arlene's Grocery on Stanton Street. Plus I still got the occasional call when he and Amy were fighting. "I want to come home." But I think New York had become his home—to the extent a person like Ryan ever has a home in the conventional sense. He was now fully installed in the East Village/Lower East Side scene. His Manhattanization was complete: NC Ryan had become NYC Ryan.

Now, on the night before my wedding, I found him and Amy in a bar in downtown Blowing Rock. "What are you doing?" I said to Ryan. "You were supposed to be at the rehearsal dinner."

"I had to take a nap," he said, hunched over his drink. "I was jet-lagged because of the flight from New York to Charlotte."

I laughed. "You can't get jet lag without leaving a time zone." He'd obviously been out late in New York the night before. "Ryan," I said, "jet lag is when you fly east and west." I clinked my beer against his. "*Hungover* is when you fly north and south."

They followed us to a bar, where we were having a late night party. Ryan played a few songs acoustic. The next day, at the actual ceremony, he dutifully wore his tux. But he changed out of it as soon as he possibly could.

The year 1999 was winding to a close, and to celebrate the end of the millennium, Whiskeytown booked a New Year's Eve show at the Cat's Cradle in Chapel Hill. The gig would be the band's only proper show of the year. The plan was to play the two full-length albums—*Faithless Street* and *Strangers Almanac*—in order, in their entirety.

Meanwhile, the fate of the new record was more uncertain than ever. By now it was clear that the Universal/PolyGram merger was bad news for Outpost Records. Its original parent company, Geffen, was going to be downsized and reorganized into a new subsidiary of Universal/PolyGram called Interscope Geffen A&M. Amid all the shuffling, Outpost would be shuttered. Whiskeytown no longer had a label to call home, so *Pneumonia* was a record with no company to release it. Bootleg copies of the album were floating around, and lots of critics recognized the creative leap forward that it was. However, with no label to manufacture and market it, and with Ryan now actively pursuing a solo career (and Caitlin showing solo aspirations, too), I was getting more and more convinced that even if *Pneumonia* eventually did come out, there would no longer be a Whiskeytown in existence to support it. Frank Callari—who was now fully on board as Ryan's manager—had his hands full.

In the weeks leading up to the Cat's Cradle show, I was back on the road with Mandy Moore. One day, when we were in San Jose, I got a second call from Jay Wilson asking if my schedule had cleared up and was I now available to tour manage Train. My obligations *had* lessened. My wedding was over. I was totally out of the picture as far as managing Ryan was concerned. Whiskeytown had zero gigs booked for 2000. There was talk of doing an SXSW show, but it was anybody's guess if the band would still be together come March. My only commitment was to Mandy, and with her I was still the utility guy, not the tour manager. Leaving Mandy and her family would be sad because we all got along so well. In fact, Stephanie and I had invited them to Thanksgiving dinner at our house. But the Train gig would be a bump in responsibility and pay. I took it. I flew back to Raleigh, got on the bus with Train, and I ended up working with them for the next thirteen years.

On one of my first days out with Train, the hotel lobby call was scheduled for 5:30 a.m. I arrived in the lobby at 5:32 to find the five of them sitting there, staring at me in disgust like, *Where the fuck have you been?* After spending three years with people who too often acted like success was owed them, it was a refreshing change to be with such determined—and yes, extremely punctual—dudes. Pat Monahan was a powerful singer, and his work ethic won me over. Train didn't just work hard, they *wanted* to work hard.

I dialed Avenue A to talk to Ryan a few times that fall and early winter, but he'd become more difficult to reach. One day, I told him I had taken the Train job. "That's probably just a bunch of Whole Foods and carrot juice, right?" he said. He kind of nailed it.

As New Year's Eve approached, I knew I'd have to miss the Cat's Cradle show. Train had booked two gigs that night, one in Atlanta and one in Birmingham. While I was gone, Ryan and Mike Daly stayed at my house in Durham and motored around the Triangle in my hatchback. Cat's Cradle ended up being the only Whiskeytown show after the release of *Strangers Almanac* that I didn't see.

Early morning. New Year's Day. The calendar digits had spun from 1999 to 2000 without incident. The computers didn't melt down. The planes didn't drop from the sky. Out in Birmingham, five hundred miles southwest of Cat's Cradle, I thought about what I'd missed back in Chapel Hill. I hadn't quit or been fired. There'd been no epic dustup. I had just slipped away. Whiskeytown was no longer a band any more than the replica town from the movie *Blazing Saddles* was really a town, all fake storefronts and empty streets.

Population: zero. But my guess was that for one night in the Triangle, everything felt good again. The way breaking up can feel good in its finality. The way unplugging the ventilator can bring peace and relief.

On Avenue A, the Ryan/Amy relationship was also falling apart. They'd been on-again, off-again for a long time, but by early 2000, the fights he'd sometimes call me about were getting more frequent and more serious. They decided to move out and split up. Amy would find another place in New York, and Ryan—for the short term, anyway—would move back to North Carolina.

At the same time, Stephanie and I were planning on moving *to* New York. We'd always wanted to live there, and now that we were married but still didn't have kids, the time was right. We started making frequent trips up I-95 and through the Holland Tunnel to search for an apartment.

One of these trips coincided with Ryan's move out of Avenue A. We volunteered to help load his stuff out and drive him back down South. Pulling up to the curb in an empty cargo van, I remembered the time Ryan and Amy had walked me around their place on Christopher Street, how happy and proud they were. Now the whole scene was depressing. While Amy watched, Stephanie and I carried Ryan's few belongings out of the apartment and into the van. As we pulled into traffic and drove along Tompkins Square Park, I looked out the sideview mirror. Their now-unwanted couch was sitting right where we left it, at the Avenue A curb.

Ryan rode in the cargo area. There were no seats back there. No seat belts. Instead, he sat on top of a guitar amplifier. He rode in that masochistic way—no headrest, no lumbar support—the full 525 miles home to the Raleigh.

CHAPTER
19

For a few weeks after leaving New York, Ryan stored his possessions at my house, but his base of operations steadily shifted west to Nashville, home of Callari's office. Before long he relocated there. When he visited North Carolina, he'd stay with Van Alston, owner of the Comet, who lived in Raleigh proper—not out in the Durham suburbs.

Then it was March. And in the music business March means the SXSW music festival. Ryan and Whiskeytown were scheduled to make a few appearances. Ryan would play a handful of solo showcases, and the band would get together for a couple of gigs. Callari asked if I would travel to Austin to do the shows. I knew he was only asking me because he needed me. I was familiar with everybody, all their personalities and tendencies. He wasn't. I hesitated at first, still irate with him because he'd opted out of the comanagement deal. But I was loyal to Ryan and the band. Plus I didn't have a previous obligation with Train. So I said yes. In Austin, I met up with the lineup they had cobbled together for the week: Ryan, Caitlin, Mike Daly, Brad Rice, Danny Kurtz, and, on drums, Ray Duffey from 6 String Drag.

Four years earlier, at SXSW 1996, there'd been a major-label feeding frenzy, and Whiskeytown had sat smack in the center of the plate. They were the great alt-country hope. One hundred percent potential. Now, at SXSW 2000, with no indication that *Pneumonia* would ever see the light of day, they were the great alt-country missed opportunity. One hundred percent history. Ryan still had buzz, but it was as a solo artist. His debut *Heartbreaker*—also produced by Ethan Johns and largely inspired by Ryan's turbulent relationship with Amy, down to the inclusion of a song called "Amy"—would be released six months later. *Pneumonia* would eventually come out on Lost Highway Records (a label Frank Callari helped launch) in May of 2001, eight months after *Heartbreaker* hit stores. By then the band had broken up, officially and permanently—to the degree that anything is ever official and permanent in rock and roll. The SXSW shows were Whiskeytown's last.

When everything was finished in Austin, I drove Ryan and the band back to the hotel in the van. The next day, we all went to the airport. Ryan was flying to Nashville. Mike Daly to Jersey. Caitlin and everybody else to Raleigh. I was headed out for the next stretch of Train shows.

Whiskeytown was over. For good this time. Nobody said it, but we all knew it. The big good-bye wasn't a big good-bye. The scene at the Austin airport was just as anticlimactic as a half-assed Whiskeytown show. Somebody should have written a set list for this moment, scripted it out for maximum emotional impact. But as it was, we just parted ways.

No tears and no thank-yous. No hugs. No good lucks. No nothing.

Caitlin and Skillet were married in October. By then, Stephanie and I were living in Brooklyn, so we flew down to Raleigh to attend the celebration. Caitlin had released a solo EP called *Waltzie* two months earlier, and she and Skillet were already Triangle royalty, so their wedding was a big event on the cultural calendar. They held the reception at a downtown restaurant called Humble Pie. As Stephanie and I walked in, the first thing that struck me was how packed the place was. Musicians, artists, and scenesters standing hip to hip, sucking beers and nibbling appetizers.

From out of the throng, Ryan appeared, walking right toward me. We said hey and he pulled me aside, steering me toward the end of the bar. After flagging down the bartender, we started talking. This was the first we'd spoken in seven months, since separating at the Austin airport after SXSW. Now that he'd moved out of Amy's place, he had less reason to call me. I'd tried to call him a few times but was unable to reach him. He was busy recording and releasing *Heartbreaker*, which had come out the previous month. In the run-up to the release, Ryan did an industry thing in New York. I figured I'd stop by and say hi. It would be a good chance to catch up. So I called Frank Callari and asked if he could put Stephanie and me on the guest list. I knew full well how quickly guest lists filled up, especially in New York and double-especially when the gig was designed with suits in mind. But I assumed Callari could find a spot for me. I was wrong. Callari told me no; he couldn't get me in. Now that he held the keys to the vehicle that was Ryan Adams, Callari no longer needed me to open the doors.

Now at the reception, Ryan and I hung out at the bar for a long time. He seemed like a different person. Different from the drunken mess he'd been on the *Strangers Almanac* tour, but also different from the about-to-go-solo artist he'd been seven months earlier in Austin.

Waiting to Derail

The change in Ryan struck me like this: Imagine a buddy you knew in high school. On graduation night you hung out with him around a bonfire. He was the same pimply-faced, goofy-ass kid you'd grown up with. You watched the fire-shadows flicker on his face, a face with just enough baby fat that you could still see what he looked like as an elementary schooler. In between shotgunning beers that night, he told you he'd enlisted in the Marine Corps. He said he couldn't wait to get to basic training, but you worried that those drill instructors at Parris Island would eat him for lunch. You bro-hugged and said good-bye, and you guessed he'd probably wash out. Six months later, you saw him again. He'd survived basic. He'd lost weight, gained muscle. He stood rifle straight. His cheekbones could cut glass. Now his demeanor was serious. No more baby fat. He'd hardened into somebody else. The goofy-ass kid you once knew was still inside there somewhere, but you had to squint to see him.

That was Ryan at Caitlin and Skillet's reception. He was in a great mood. Cracking wise, being silly. But he looked older, harder. More determined and assertive. Talking with him that night, it was obvious: for the kid from Jacksonville, home of Camp Lejeune, Whiskeytown had been basic training. Now Ryan Adams was all set for deployment as a solo artist. He was in tip-top shape, ready and prepared to go it alone.

There at the bar, I told Ryan I was proud of him. I told him I was certain that his solo career was going to work out. I didn't know exactly what the Ryan solo trajectory would look like. I didn't know that he was destined for the accolades that would come over the next eighteen years—the Grammy nominations, the sold out-shows, the tremendous creative output—but I sure suspected it. My prediction from years earlier, at the Waffle House outside Nashville, would turn out be correct. Whiskeytown would be to Ryan Adams as Mudcrutch was to Tom Petty: a brief but essential first act that foreshadowed a much longer and more productive career under his own name.

I patted Ryan on the back and told him I had to take off. Stephanie and I gave our congratulations to Caitlin and Skillet, and we aimed for the exit. But then I turned around a got one last look at Ryan, who was holding court and being charming. He projected hard-earned confidence rather than drunken cockiness. When I met him, he'd been a lunatic fuck-up. Now he was grown up—almost. There'd still be mistakes and missed shows, drunken Internet posts and trivial arguments. He'd still dazzle an audience one night and disappoint them the next. But he was becoming the person we all hoped he'd become. And I was glad I'd had the chance to guide him a little farther down the path.

I turned toward the door and walked out. My work was done.

EPILOGUE

The events depicted in this book are based on my firsthand experience, notes I took at the time, conversations I've had over the years with the principal characters, and, most recently, interviews with band and crew members. I spoke with every musician who played in Whiskeytown, every crew member who toured with us, all the bus drivers, all living managers, and many of the record company people. There was only one major exception: Ryan himself. I reached out to him personally and through his attorney, but Ryan made it clear that he wasn't interested in participating. Given that he's always looking forward to the next project, it doesn't surprise me that he would be reluctant to discuss the past.

One of my favorite things about writing this book was catching up with everyone who lived it, and I want to thank them all for sharing their memories with me. The cast of characters has moved on with life after Whiskeytown, and many have done great and interesting things.

After Whiskeytown finally broke up, I started tour-managing Train, and we played all over the world. Thirteen productive years later, I left Train to take on a new challenge, moving to Nashville to become an artist manager at Crush Music, where I worked with Ashley Monroe and Striking Matches. After the Nashville office closed in late 2015, I went back to tour-managing, working with Sia, Dashboard Confessional, and Third Eye Blind. I'm currently the tour manager for one of my favorite bands, Weezer. I'm also an adjunct professor at Segue 61 / Catawba College, and I still write and perform with Judas Bullethead, the rock duo I formed with Jeff Clayton from ANTiSEEN. I live in Nashville with Stephanie; our daughter, Sophie; our niece, Ana; and a sweet beagle named Lola.

Here's what everybody else is up to these days (in alphabetical order):

Ryan Adams became one of the most important artists of the last decade. He continues to release albums at breakneck speed and sells out venues on multiple continents. The one place he refuses to play is North Carolina, having not done a show in the Tar Heel State in the last thirteen years. He lives in Los Angeles.

ANTiSEEN continues to record and tour all over the world. The band has released over ninety records to date, and their latest album, *Obstinate*, came out in summer 2017. Founding guitarist Joe Young passed away suddenly in 2014 of a heart attack at the age of fifty-three. Singer Jeff Clayton and I are working on a documentary that we will film during the band's thirty-fifth anniversary show in late 2018.

Jeff Caler (front-of-house sound) continued touring, mixing for Seven Mary Three, D Generation, Train, and an occasional Ryan Adams solo show. He currently owns an insurance and financial services business in Phoenix, where he lives with his wife, Rachel, and two daughters, Charlie and Kate.

Frank Callari (artist manager) went on to manage Ryan's solo career. He also worked at Lost Highway records as Senior VP of A&R. He died in Nashville in 2007 at the age of fifty-five.

Caitlin Cary went on to release three highly acclaimed solo albums, a duets record with Thad Cockrell, two albums with "super group" Tres Chicas, and EPs with the Small Ponds. Touring nationally and internationally, Caitlin has shared stages with Lyle Lovett, Mary Chapin Carpenter, Steve Earle, Alejandro Escovedo, and many more. While several of her bands remain active, she now focuses primarily on making visual art, a form of sewn fabric collage she calls "Needle Print." She works from a studio at Raleigh's Artspace, and her work is widely collected in the Triangle region and beyond. You can view her work at www.caitlincary.com. Whiskeytown brought Caitlin and Skillet together, and they remain happily married, the "parents" of three super-fun doggies.

John "JC" Clark (front-of-house sound) resides in Hillsborough, North Carolina, and has two superlative young'uns, Eliza and Henry. He got off the road, settled down a bit, and now owns and operates Green Build General Contracting. He also plays the guitar in a few local bands, records music in his studio, and is staring down the barrel of his fiftieth birthday. His favorite quote: "We may be lost, but we're making good time."

Scott Clayton (booking agent) parted ways with Whiskeytown but continued as an agent at the Progressive Global Agency before moving to Creative Artists Agency in 2000. In late 2017, Scott made a move over to William Morris Endeavor to build out a new rock division in their Nashville office. He is the agent for John Mayer, Dead & Company, Kings of Leon, My Morning Jacket, Train, Zac Brown Band, Steve Winwood, and many others. *Strangers Almanac* remains one of his favorite albums of all time. He lives in Nashville with his wife, three kids, and his dog Banjo.

Ed Crawford is still proud of Whiskeytown's performance on *Austin City Limits* and his friendship with Caitlin, Skillet, and Thomas. He has since left Chapel Hill, moving to Pittsburgh to be closer to his parents. He is not of fan of Ryan Adams, though he remembers Ace with great fondness.

D Generation split up for a time, beginning in 1999. Singer Jesse Malin's 2003 solo LP, *The Fine Art of Self Destruction*, was produced by Ryan Adams. Jesse continued to make many critically acclaimed albums, including *Glitter in the Gutter*, which features "Broken Radio," a duet with Bruce Springsteen. In 2008, the band reunited with all the original members, and after an ill-fated attempt to make a record with Ryan Adams producing, they released their fourth album, *Nothing is Everywhere*, in 2016.

Mike Daly continues to have a successful career as a record producer, songwriter, and A&R executive, working with such artists as Jason Mraz, Lana Del Rey, and Imagine Dragons. He has spoken as a panelist at the SXSW Music Festival and at Berklee College of Music. He has also performed on numerous television programs, such as *Austin City Limits*, *The Tonight Show with Jay Leno Show*, and *Good Morning America*. In 2008, he released his first book, *Time Flies When You're in a Coma: The Wisdom of the Metal Gods*, published by Penguin. He currently lives in Los Angeles.

Ace Davis (merch and guitar tech) went on to tech for Dishwalla. He bounced around North Carolina for a while, working at many different restaurants. For over a year, he was homeless in Raleigh, sleeping under a Korean Church a few blocks from Sadlack's Heroes. Ace currently lives and cooks on a cruise ship in Hawaii, claims to have two Hawaiian girlfriends, and is most likely catching a buzz as we speak.

Uncle Donnie (bus driver) is still out there, driving a tour bus and living outside Nashville. Hopefully, he's still enjoying his hash browns with holiday sauce.

Ray Duffey only played one concert with Whiskeytown (SXSW 2000), save for the impromptu jams at Park County. Since then, he has toured with Caitlin Cary, among other Triangle bands, and continued his long musical friendships with Steve Grothmann (Countdown Quartet) and, of course, Kenny Roby (6 String Drag,

Mercy Filter). Still drumming (Pork & Beans Brass Band), Ray teaches Furniture Design at Herron School of Art & Design in Indianapolis and maintains a studio practice (www.rayduffey.com) there with his wife, Meredith Brickell, and son, Clyde.

Skillet Gilmore continued touring with bands for several years before coming to his senses. He now enjoys a semitenured, possibly permanent position as drummer in the World's Best Worst Rock Band, the Vibekillers. They play twice a year or so, assuming they can get booked at Slim's in Raleigh. Skillet has gone on to become a nationally recognized graphic artist and printmaker, designing work for artists such as Lucinda Williams, Gillian Welch, Patterson Hood, and many others. He lives in South Raleigh with Caitlin and their three dogs.

Danny Kurtz went on to play in many more bands including MSRP (Mike Spence Rock Project, which includes D Generation member Richard Bacchus) and the reunited Backsliders. He's currently employed in the publishing industry as a graphic designer. Danny is happily married to Jennifer Warren Kurtz and lives in Raleigh with their two dogs, Barney and Coltrane, and cat, Peaches.

Chris Laney went on to play with several bands after Whiskeytown, including Sleep Tight, Abeline Strip, Pellum Blue, and National Era. He is currently a successful businessman, living in Carrolton, Georgia, with his wife, Christie, and their three children, Liam, Adeline, and Sawyer.

Travis Langley (front-of-house sound) continues to work in the production business as an audio engineer and system designer. He is currently Senior Audio Engineer for a corporate production company based in St. Louis, working out of their Kansas City office. He lives in Shawnee, Kansas, with his beautiful wife, Katie, and two sons, Miles and Owen. His ears are still ringing from his Whiskeytown days.

Mandy Moore continued her music career, recording six albums from 1999 to 2009. She has also appeared in dozens of films and television shows. She married Ryan Adams in Savannah, Georgia, in March 2009. They divorced in 2016. Not long after, Mandy became the star of the hit NBC show *This Is Us*. Her philanthropy extends to many causes. She lives in Los Angeles.

Bruce Neese (front-of-house sound) continued traveling the world as tour manager and live sound engineer for Tonic, Hank III, Fates Warning, Laura Izibor, and others. He quit the road in 2010 to work on his own music. Bruce currently lives near Athens, Georgia, where he owns an organic farm and an online vintage retail store, Mid Century Mod One.

Andy Nelson (Universal Records) moved to Nashville in 2001 to work for Lost Highway Records and put out albums by Ryan Adams, Whiskeytown, Johnny Cash, Willie Nelson, Tift Merritt, the Jayhawks, Lucinda Williams, Timothy B. Schmit, Hayes Carll, Ryan Bingham, Black Joe Lewis, and others until its demise in 2012. He's currently back home in the Pacific Northwest, where he enjoys gardening and thinking about exercising with his wife, Sonja, who works for *No Depression*, and their two Americana-hating kids,

Jack and Lily. Andy is the Vinyl Czar at Easy Street Records, where he continues his search for a copy of the first Rush album on Moon Records.

Jenni Snyder Renshaw went on to play with several bands throughout the 1990s and 2000s, including Grand National, Spider Bags, Jimmy and the Teasers, Calico Haunts, Grinder Nova, and the Neil Diamond Allstars. She has established a successful career as a hair stylist/business owner. She lives in Decatur, Georgia, with her husband, Adam Renshaw, a film/TV producer and professional drummer. An avid runner, she has competed in many races in the United States and Canada

Brad Rice played in Ryan's solo band from 2001 to 2004. Then he toured with Tift Merritt for her Tambourine record and made two records and toured with Son Volt. In 2007, he joined Keith Urban's touring band for three years. Since 2010, Rice has played and recorded with German superstar Marius Mueller Westernhagen. He has also recorded with Ray Wylie Hubbard, Will Hoge, Peter Case, and Javier Escovedo, among others. Brad released a solo recording in 2005, *Karma Bed*, and has new material coming out in 2018.

Chris Roldan (artist manager) didn't want to work in an industry where *Strangers Almanac* was not quadruple platinum, so he got out of the music business entirely and went into something much less stressful: film and television. He has worked as an editor on two Oscar-nominated films, *Boyhood* and *Tree of Life*. He has edited television shows for Discovery Channel, TNT, Lifetime, and TLC, as well as award-winning documentaries and music videos. He is an adjunct professor of advanced editing at the University of Texas, where he was recognized in 2015 as one of the top ten professors on campus. He has been married to his beautiful wife, Mia, for over twenty years, and they have two children, Desmond and Darby. He still has about fifty CDs of *Strangers Almanac* and still gets PTSD when he hears Ryan's voice coming through the PA system in Home Depot. He's waiting for just the right time to put the picture Ryan drew of him on eBay.

Mike Santoro recorded with Caitlin Cary on her solo debut CD *While You Weren't Looking* and was also a member of her touring band in England and Scotland. He later joined 34 Satellite, recording two CDs and touring nationally. His other work includes recordings with Amy Allison, Robert McCreedy (Volebeats), Mary McBride, the Pink Delicates, and Demolition String Band. He recently recorded a second CD with songwriter Eric Athey, scheduled for release in 2018. Mike lives in the Philadelphia area with his wife, Laura, and their dog, cats, and fish.

Debbie Southwood-Smith (A&M Records) ended up signing some great rock-and-roll bands. At A&M, she had a hit record with Monster Magnet's *Powertrip*. As a VP of A&R at Interscope Records, she signed the Yeah Yeah Yeahs and, in her opinion, one of the world's greatest rock-and-roll bands, Queens of the Stone Age. Debbie left the music business and her beloved one-bedroom West Village apartment in 2005. After earning a master's degree in education, she spent eight years teaching high school English in the inner city. She is a certified yoga instructor and an avid practitioner. Currently, Debbie lives in New Jersey, where she continues to downward dog, walk her dogs, and spend quite a bit of time talking about rock and roll.

Jenni Sperandeo (artist manager) continued with Jacknife management and promotion through 1999. She moved on to work at both indie and major labels in New York and Los Angeles, playing key roles with Drive-By Truckers, the Kooks, and Fitz and the Tantrums, among others. She was named president of LA-based indie label Dangerbird Records in 2012, signing and developing a diverse roster of artists that includes Butch Walker, Slothrust, Juiceboxxx, the Frights, T. Hardy Morris, and others. She is certain that Ryan Adams wouldn't walk across the street to spit on her if she were on fire, but she's cool with that.

Steven Terry recorded a plethora of material with Ryan Adams and Mike Daly—later used in bootlegs and demos for future Whiskeytown and Ryan albums. In 2001, while opening his music venue in Brooklyn (Southpaw), he joined forces with some lads and formed the legendary rock band the Damnwells. After years of touring and record-making with the Damnwells, he met his soon-to-be wife Alysia and started baby making, all while still recording, touring, and business making. He currently lives in Brooklyn and West Virginia with Alysia and their children, Rowan and Salem, and owns a restaurant, Salem's Hour, named after his daughter. He still plays and records with anyone who asks.

Phil Wandscher drove to Seattle in 1998 and planted his flag in the old fishing area of Ballard. He soon met songwriter Jesse

Sykes and formed the band Jesse Sykes and the Sweet Hereafter. They are currently working on their fifth album. From singing on the doom metal record *Altar* to playing guitar on Marissa Nadler's *July* to moonlighting as Jon Langford's sideman, Phil continues to contribute to the musical fabric in a special kind of way.

Tim Wendt (bus driver) and his brother formed a band in the late 1990s called "the Wendt Brothers" and released a few singles. He retired from driving a bus in 2000 and moved from Nashville to Kansas City. He began working as a financial/investment advisor with Ameriprise Financial in 2003 and is now in his fifteenth year with the company. He has two daughters, Skye and Jailyn, and is enjoying being a dad and small business owner. He says other than being a dad to his daughters, his time in the entertainment industry and the relationships he formed there are still some of the best days of his life.

Mark Williams (Outpost Records) climbed the music-biz corporate ladder to become president of A&R at Columbia Records. In early 2018, he left that position. He lives in Los Angeles.

Jon Wurster continues to play music for a living, recording and touring with Superchunk, the Mountain Goats, and Bob Mould. He is one half of the Scharpling & Wurster comedy duo.

The End.
Until Ryan decides to do a Whiskeytown reunion tour.

ACKNOWLEDGMENTS

Our deepest gratitude to the following people for helping this book come to life:

Joseph Craig and all of our friends at Skyhorse Publishing.

John Rudolph and everyone at Dystel, Goderich, and Bourret.

Nick Powell for nearly reaching the end of the Internet trying to keep up with Ryan Adams news.

Additionally, from Thomas O'Keefe:

I'd like to thank Stephanie for her love and hard work, and for taking care of everything while I was gone on tour over the last twenty-six years.

Sophie and Ana for their love and support.

Joe Oestreich for being such a great partner, leading us through this project and answering dozens of rambling 10:00 p.m. phone calls.

Andy Nelson for suggesting back in 1997 that I write this book.

All the members of Whiskeytown, including the musicians, crew, drivers, managers, and record company people. We were the first believers.

Last but not least, thanks to Ryan Adams for giving me a front row seat. It all worked out—exactly as we talked about at that late night Nashville Waffle House dinner so long ago.

And from Joe Oestreich:

I'd like to thank Kate, Beckett, and Ellie for their love, patience, and enthusiasm. And many thanks to Thomas O'Keefe for his deep well of support over the years. This partnership started in 1997, on a night when my band Watershed played the Brewery. Thomas heard us cover Cheap Trick's "He's a Whore," and his ears perked up. Ryan got bored and disappeared into the Comet.

NOTES

Chapter 1

—During the 1996 SXSW music festival, at a panel called "Americana,"—

Raoul Hernandez, "'Americana' Panel/Go to Blazes," *Austin Chronicle*, accessed November 22, 2016, http://www.austinchronicle.com/issues/vol15/issue29/music.funhouse.html.

Chapter 2

—he told the *Cleveland Plain Dealer* that he hated the alt-country label—

Douglas Fulmer, "Whiskeytown to Change Poison for Next Album," *Cleveland Plain Dealer*, June 20, 1997, 26.

—"I could give a fuck about being a country band"—

David Menconi, *Ryan Adams: Losering, a Story of Whiskeytown* (Austin: University of Texas Press, 2012), 83.

—**"Much of it was highly energized and entertaining"**—
Douglas Fulmer, "Roots Rockers Energized, Entertaining," *Cleveland Plain Dealer*, June 28, 1997, 5B.

—**It would draw upwards of 750,000 fans and feature hundreds of bands**—
Attendance estimate based on information gleaned from the following source:
Bobby Tanzilo, "The History of Summerfest," *On Milwaukee*, June 29, 2017, accessed July 31, 2017, https://onmilwaukee.com/seasonal/festivals/articles/summerfest50.html.

Chapter 3

—**the most humiliating night of her life**—
and

—*I am truly sorry you have to endure how i feel*—
David Menconi, *Ryan Adams: Losering, a Story of Whiskeytown* (Austin: University of Texas Press, 2012), 103–104.

Chapter 4

—**"an eclectic space that's always thriving with live DJs and emerging artists."**—
—"Raleigh Bar WXYZ," *Aloft Raleigh*, accessed February 4, 2018, http://www.aloftraleigh.com/raleigh-bars.

—**the Raleigh-Durham-Chapel Hill metropolitan statistical area**—

All population and census data taken from:
U.S. Bureau of the Census. *State and Metropolitan Area Data Book 1997–98* (5th edition), Washington, DC, 1998.

—**"ground zero for insurgent country"**—
and

—**home base of alt-country**—
David Menconi, "Alt-country 'Tis of Thee," *The News & Observer*, July 27, 1997, G1.

—**country was merely the starting point**—
Jeffrey Lee Puckett, "Music Reviews," *USA Today*, August 15, 1997.

—***Rolling Stone*'s three-star review**—
David Menconi, *Ryan Adams: Losering, a Story of Whiskeytown* (Austin: University of Texas Press, 2012), 99.

—**A review in the *Austin American-Statesman***—
"Whiskeytown Goes Down Smooth," *Austin American-Statesman*, July 29, 1997, E1.

—**Whiskeytown open to charges that they sold out . . .**—
Andy Langer, "No Expectations," *Austin Chronicle*, September 5, 1997, accessed October 3, 2016, http://www.austinchronicle.com/music/19970905/518354/.

—**"authenticity can be measured in different ways.**—
Jonathan Perry, "No Depressions: America's New Roots Pioneers," *Boston Phoenix*, September 18-25, 1997, accessed October 7, 2016, http://www.bostonphoenix.com/archive/music/97/09/18/NO_DEPRESSION.html.

—. . . this record is a smart kid just making stuff up."—
David Menconi, "Alt-country 'Tis of Thee," *News & Observer*,
July 27, 1997, G1.

—Outpost Recordings' Mark Williams also heard the criticism—
Ibid.

—. . . eighteen-year-old Ryan was practicing with Lazy Stars—
David Menconi, *Ryan Adams: Losering, a Story of Whiskeytown*
(Austin: University of Texas Press, 2012), 23–24.

—According to Williams, Scott "immediately reacted to the
songwriting . . . —
David Menconi, "Whiskeytown Has Songs to Spare,"
Billboard, June 28, 1997, 10.

—Ryan told *No Depression*'s Peter Blackstock . . . —
Peter Blackstock, "Whiskeytown: Falling Down, Standing
Up," *No Depression*, June 30, 1997, accessed November 22, 2016,
http://nodepression.com/article/whiskeytown-falling-down-
standing.

—Ryan really did do the drugs and drink the liquor and write the
songs. —
David Menconi, *Ryan Adams: Losering, a Story of Whiskeytown*
(Austin: University of Texas Press, 2012), 109-110.

—A review in the *Houston Chronicle* seemed to believe it . . . —
Steve Crawford, "Recordings," *Houston Chronicle*, August 17,
1997, 6.

Chapter 5

—A review of the show in *Rolling Stone* read . . . —
"Live Report: Whiskeytown in New York," *Rolling Stone*, August 14, 1997, accessed November 2, 2016, http://www. rollingstone.com/music/news/live-report-whiskeytown-in-new-york-19970814.

—Gaurino walked with Ryan to a liquor store . . . —
Mark Gaurino, "Waiting to Derail: Ryan Adams Pays the Price for Telling the Truth," *Daily Herald*, September 5, 1997, 4.

—A review in the *Chicago Sun-Times* . . . —
Mary Houlihan-Skilton, "A Loaded Singer Dilutes Whiskeytown's Promise," *Chicago Sun-Times*, August 26, 1997, 34.

— . . . when his story of the night described Whiskeytown as "loose" . . . —
Mark Gaurino, "Waiting to Derail: Ryan Adams Pays the Price for Telling the Truth," *Daily Herald*, September 5, 1997, 4.

— "Our band is like a place you come to," . . . —
Ibid.

—Ryan would write on Facebook that Anne "was always friendly" . . . —
Kim Bell, "Woman Dead, Father Injured in Webster Groves House Fire," *St. Louis Post-Dispatch*, April 9, 2015, accessed July 31, 2017, http://www.stltoday.com/news/local/crime-and-courts/woman-dead-father-injured-in-webster-groves-house-fire/article_8279c729-1997-5f75-aa79-0c656b949f4f.html.

Chapter 6

—"Whiskeytown burned through an amazing set . . . —

Malcolm Mayhew, "Dark Room, Gray Mood, Brilliant Show for Whiskeytown," *Fort Worth Star-Telegram*, September 7, 1997, 4.

Chapter 7

—I didn't know it yet, but Skillet would later say . . . —

Gilbert Garcia, "Town Without Pity," *Phoenix New Times*, January 29, 1998, accessed January 17, 2017, http://www.phoenixnewtimes.com/music/town-without-pity-6422441.

—As he'd later tell the *Phoenix New Times*,—

Gilbert Garcia, "Town Without Pity," *Phoenix New Times*, January 29, 1998, accessed January 17, 2017, http://www.phoenixnewtimes.com/music/town-without-pity-6422441.

—*No Depression*'s Grant Alden would later rave about the show . . . —

Grant Alden, "Whiskeytown—Exit/In (Nashville, TN)," *No Depression*, October 31, 1997, accessed November 2, 2016, http://nodepression.com/live-review/whiskeytown-exitin-nashville-tn.

Chapter 8

— . . . telling a reporter from Pittsburgh: "They're going to get shown up.—

Scott Mervis, "The Nirvana of Country-Rock?" *Pittsburgh Post-Gazette*, October 21, 1997, D-3.

—"We'd rather hit every night," . . . —
Jim McGuinness, "Distilled Variations—A Whiskeytown Changeover," *New Jersey Record*, October 17, 1997, 37.

Chapter 9

—"I live in places the way Tom Waits lives in places," . . . —
Chris Riemenschneider, "A Tale of Two Bands (and One City)—Whiskeytown, 6 String Drag Follow Alt-country Train Out of Raleigh," *Austin American-Statesman*, January 22, 1998, 12.

—". . . half band, half soap-opera."—
Dave Simpson, "Ryan Adams: 'Things Got Broken and I Couldn't Fix Them.'" *Guardian*, September 22, 2011, accessed July 31, 2017, https://www.theguardian.com/music/2011/sep/22/ryan-adams-things-got-broken.

—In the 1997 edition of the *Village Voice*'s "Pazz and Jop" poll . . . —
Robert Christgau, "The 1997 Pazz & Jop Critics Poll," accessed July 31, 2017, https://www.robertchristgau.com/xg/pnj/pjres97.php.

—"I'm usually about four or five steps ahead of myself," . . . —
Yon Lambert, "Turmoil Feeds Whiskeytown's Rise to Top of Alt-country Heap," *The State*, November 14, 1997, 12.

—"I think it'd be great to make a couple of records a year," . . . —
Kenn Rodriguez, "Whiskeytown Hard to Put on Map," *Albuquerque Journal*, January 23, 1998, E12.

Chapter 10

—"The only reason they're playing is because we're letting 'em,"
. . . —

Malcolm Mayhew, "Whiskeytown Take It to The 'Limits," *Fort Worth Star-Telegram*, January 23, 1998, 7.

—" . . . fast gaining a reputation as one of the most reckless figures in nineties rock."—

J. Freedom du Lac, "Whiskeytown's Singer Savors Life to the Last Drop," *Sacramento Bee*, February 6, 1998, TK16.

Chapter 11

—"Whiskeytown is one of the most promising of the new alternative country bands . . . —

Patrick MacDonald, "Whiskeytown at Showbox Fails to Live up to Promise," *Seattle Times*, February 16, 1998, E5.

Chapter 12

— "I don't give a fuck about our audience. I just make the doughnuts. . .. —

Gilbert Garcia, "Town Without Pity," *Phoenix New Times*, January 29, 1998, accessed January 17, 2017, http://www.phoenixnewtimes.com/music/town-without-pity-6422441.

Chapter 13

—"Whiskeytown seems to be this month's pick among college radio . . . —

Nick Carter, "Whiskeytown Distills Rock to a Countrified Essence," *Milwaukee Journal Sentinel*, March 26, 1998, 8.

—. . . it would hit number one and stay there for seven weeks . . .
—

Billboard Charts Archive, "Alternative Songs—1998 Archive," *Billboard*, accessed August 1, 2017, http://www.billboard.com/archive/charts/1998/alternative-songs.

—"Adams seemed lower-key and more vulnerable . . . —

Paul Sexton, "Country of the Soul," *The Times of London*, May 11, 1998.

Chapter 14

— . . . Ryan would publicly admit to suffering from Ménière's disease . . . —

Ian Drew, "Ryan Adams Opens Up About Tragic Ear Disease," *US Weekly*, October 21, 2011, accessed August 1, 2017, http://www.usmagazine.com/entertainment/news/ryan-adams-opens-up-about-tragic-ear-disease-20112110.

Chapter 16

—"Whiskeytown played a remarkable show . . . —

Malcolm Mayhew, "Smartly Re-tooled Whiskeytown Goes Down Smooth, Easy," *Fort Worth Star-Telegram*, September 20, 1998, 9.